REDEFINING REMEDIAL EDUCATION

CROOM HELM SERIES ON SPECIAL EDUCATIONAL
NEEDS: POLICY, PRACTICES AND SOCIAL ISSUES

General Editor: Len Barton, Westhill College,
Birmingham,

SPECIAL EDUCATION AND SOCIAL INTERESTS
Edited by Len Barton and Sally Tomlinson

COPING WITH SPECIAL NEEDS:
A GUIDE FOR NEW TEACHERS
Geof Sewell

REDEFINING REMEDIAL EDUCATION

HAZEL BINES

CROOM HELM
London • Sydney • Dover, New Hampshire

© 1986 Hazel Bines
Croom Helm Ltd, Provident House, Burrell Row,
Beckenham, Kent, BR3 1AT
Croom Helm Australia Pty Ltd, Suite 4, 6th Floor,
64-76 Kippax Street, Surry Hills, NSW 2010, Australia

British Library Cataloguing in Publication Data

Bines, Hazel
    Redefining remedial education.
    1. Learning disabilities — Great Britain
    2. Remedial teaching 3. Education,
    Secondary — Great Britain
    I. Title
    371.9'0941   LC4706.G7
        ISBN 0-7099-3984-1
        ISBN 0-7099-5028-4 Pbk

Croom Helm, 27 South Main Street,
Wolfeboro, New Hampshire 03894-2069, USA

Library of Congress Cataloging in Publication Data

Bines, Hazel.
    Redefining remedial education.

    Bibliography: p.
    1. Remedial teaching. 2. Learning disabled
children—Education (secondary)—Great Britain.
I. Title.
LB1029.R4B52   1986   371.9   86-8901
ISBN 0-7099-3984-1
ISBN 0-7099-5028-4 (pbk.)

Printed and bound in Great Britain
by Billing & Sons Limited, Worcester.

CONTENTS

INTRODUCTION

This book is concerned with the new approaches to
remedial education which have been mooted during the
last decade and with some of their theoretical and
practical implications. Its major aim is to
engender further debate and discussion on policies
and practice, by drawing on a number of research
studies and perspectives, including sociological
approaches to remedial and special education. Such
approaches have rarely been used in relation to
remedial education but it is hoped to demonstrate
their relevance and importance. There is an
orientation to practice, not least because of the
many years I have spent in schools and classrooms.
However it is also considered that the divorce
between 'theory' and 'practice' has always been
dubious, and that 'theoretical' issues and analysis
can help with the understanding of the content,
implications and consequences of both routine and
innovatory practice. A number of theoretical
problems are therefore discussed. Although there
are some criticisms of ideas and practices, these
are offered in a spirit of commitment to
improvements in remedial education and with an
optimistic contention that reflexivity is not the
prerogative of sociologists alone.

The use of terminology in a time of change is
problematic. It was decided to use the terms
'remedial education', 'remedial teacher' and 'pupils
with learning difficulties' although they are far
from ideal and despite the increasingly wide use of
new terms like 'special educational needs', because
of their specific focus and their utility as readily
understood terms. Their many limitations and
implications are, of course, recognised.

There are many debts which need to be
acknowledged, not least to those writers and

1

researchers whose ideas and findings I have used and explored. I would also particularly like to thank those teachers who took part in my research and gave their time, their interest and their insights. This book would not have been written without their contribution. I would also like to thank officers and advisers of the LEA concerned for their time and help and for permission to carry out the research. I would also like to acknowledge the help of those colleagues and friends who have talked and worked with me in schools or who have guided my training and education as a teacher and as a researcher and thus have also made a contribution to this book. My thanks too, to Len Barton, for his editorial advice and encouragement and to a necessarily anonymous referee for very valuable comments. I would also particularly like to thank my husband Steve for his support. Finally I would like to dedicate this book to my parents, Ted and Connie French, whose lifelong commitment to the eradication of disadvantage, injustice and inequality has been the touchstone for my own and for my ensuing involvement with the area of education which is the focus of this book.

Chapter One

THE CONTEXT OF CHANGE

Remedial education has traditionally been a
neglected aspect of secondary education. Surveys of
provision have consistently drawn attention to
inadequate resources, a lack of specially qualified
teachers, inappropriate or limited curricula, a
diversity of aims and objectives, the low status
accorded to many remedial teachers, their isolation
from the rest of the school and the low level of
priority and policy attention given to remedial work
(Sampson and Pumfrey, 1970, DES, 1971, Brennan,
1979, DES, 1979, DES, 1984). However a new approach
to remedial education has now been suggested, which
posits the development of 'remedial education across
the curriculum', with remedial teachers working in
partnership with subject teachers to provide a more
effective and comprehensive provision for pupils
with learning difficulties. In addition, following
the Warnock Report (DES, 1978) and the 1981
Education Act, more attention is being given to the
education of pupils with special needs.
    Nevertheless, although these new developments
would seem to offer a considerable potential in
respect of changing the traditional isolation and
low status of remedial teaching, many aspects of the
proposed new approach to, or redefinition[1] of
remedial education need further examination and
discussion. For example, consideration needs to be
given to the new demands which redefinition will
make on the knowledge and expertise of remedial
teachers and to the ways in which a new approach
will mesh with traditional policies and practice.
Then too, the development of 'remedial education
across the curriculum' and of a 'new partnership'
between subject and remedial teachers will involve
examination of curricula, teaching methods and
school organisation and will also draw remedial

3

teachers more closely into the complex network of academic and social relationships found within the secondary school. Remedial teachers will thus need a fuller understanding of mainstream educational practices, of this network of relationships and of the context which shapes and sustains them. Moreover, despite the apparent potential of this redefinition of remedial education, the legacies of traditional neglect and of traditional practice may continue to mould the direction and implementation of change. It is thus also important to consider why such a redefinition has taken place and to assess its likely outcome.

This book will be concerned with such themes. It will examine the redefinition of remedial education and consider many aspects of implementation. It will be suggested that both redefinition and its implementation cannot be examined in isolation from the wider context of secondary education or without some consideration of the features of secondary and remedial education which have given rise to such change and which may in turn influence its development. This chapter will therefore set a framework for future discussion by focusing on some of the features of traditional policy and practice in remedial education which are considered to be significant to the context of change.

THE STATUS OF REMEDIAL EDUCATION

The low and marginal status of remedial provision in many secondary schools is reflected in the peripheral position held in relation to the main aims and content of the curriculum. Remedial teachers have often been isolated from their colleagues, their skills being seen as relevant to only a small minority of pupils and divorced from the main academic life of the school. In consequence a low priority and inadequate resources have been accorded to remedial work, with both remedial teachers and their pupils being held in somewhat low esteem. This situation has given rise to much concern from remedial teachers and has generated many arguments for changes in policy and practice. In 1975, for example, Paul Widlake, the then President of the National Association for Remedial Education (NARE)[2], argued that notwithstanding the progress achieved since the Second World War, when remedial provision scarcely

4

existed, the status of remedial education must be improved. Remedial teachers should 'come out from the cloakrooms and under the stage' and take their places alongside other colleagues. Moreover, 'the ability to teach less-able children must be seen as a skill equal to that of the good subject teacher' with adequate working conditions being provided to achieve high professional standards (Widlake, 1975, p.107). Ian Galletley made a similar point in an article arguing for changes in remedial education. Pointing out that remedial teachers were too often thought of as

> good-hearted, well-intentioned, a sound 'general subjects' type, the sort whom head teachers call the 'salt of the earth' and keep on scale one for ever
> (1976,p.149)

he suggested that remedial teachers should work far more closely with other colleagues to avoid the isolation and low status of separate remedial provision. Such calls for change have been taken up by many remedial teachers. However the degree to which status has improved remains open to question. A recent survey found teachers of 'slow learners' still over-represented on Scale One in comparison with the rest of the teaching force whilst teachers in charge of such provision were still often not involved in major policy decisions (Clunies-Ross and Wimhurst, 1983). That remedial teachers and their pupils are still very much 'out of sight and out of mind' as far as other colleagues are concerned (Lee, 1984) remains the experience of perhaps many remedial teachers in secondary schools, an experience borne out by evidence from recent surveys by HMI. Sadly, such surveys continue to indicate that the quality of work with less able pupils remains one of the most unsatisfactory aspects of secondary schools (DES, 1984, 1985a). Thus it could be suggested that remedial education does not enjoy the status and concomitant esteem and resource allocation which ought seemingly to be accorded to a field of provision which is concerned with a significant proportion of the school population[3] and which has much to contribute to equalising educational opportunities and achievements within school. A number of reasons could be put forward for this situation. Perhaps the isolation of remedial teaching and the low level of resources often received are in part a consequence of lack of knowledge about remedial work or stem from beliefs that remedial teaching is somehow special and different. Many teachers may be reluctant to take an interest since they think they do not have the requisite specialist expertise. Thus remedial work becomes isolated and marginal to mainstream teaching activities and techniques. Lack of knowledge about remedial work may also have affected the allocation of resources and staffing in that the need for small groups, and for specialised materials and equipment, may not be fully realised by those non-specialists who may be in charge of resources and staffing. Lack of status may also be associated with the level of specialist qualifications held by remedial teachers. Clunies-Ross and Wimhurst (op.cit.) found that only half of their sample of teachers of 'slow learners' had attended a recent specialist course (p.94) and this lack of qualifications and training may have affected both credibility and promotion. It may also be significant that the majority of remedial teachers are women, who are traditionally under-represented in more senior posts (NUT,1980). Perhaps though the most crucial factors affecting the status of remedial education involve the status and situation of the pupils with which remedial education is concerned.

Pupils with learning difficulties are often seen to be 'failures', unable to cope with the learning experiences which are the focus of most school activity and which can be mastered by their peers. Given that much of the life of secondary schools tends to revolve around the demands and activities of academic work, especially examinations, pupils with learning difficulties are only too easily relegated to the edge of such life. In addition, secondary education is still dominated by a stratification of curricula which gives highest status to abstract, examinable knowledge requiring a high level of literacy (Young,1971) and thus it is perhaps not surprising that the status of pupils with learning difficulties, those who cannot apparently master such curricula, should be both low and marginal. Even the extension of accreditation and the development of new courses and examinations may have done little to change this situation and may indeed have exacerbated it. New courses which seek to be 'relevant' to daily life and which use more informal methods of assessment have come to be associated with 'less able' pupils, reinforcing their differentiation from the more 'academic' pupil whilst, as Gray, McPherson and Raffe have perceptively pointed out in their study of Scottish secondary education, the shrinking minority of pupils who do not now gain certificates (which includes many pupils with learning difficulties) have been put in a particularly invidious position, tantamount to 'exclusion from the moral community of the school' (1983,p.303).

Since remedial teachers are primarily concerned with this marginal group of pupils who receive little esteem and attention, it could be suggested that their teaching activities have tended to acquire the same low and marginal status. Such status is further grounded in and reinforced by the occupational culture of teachers. Status and claims to professional expertise in secondary schools still tend to rest largely in the teaching of 'subjects' rather than pastoral work or pedagogic skills (Hargreaves,1980). Remedial teachers, who are largely concerned with the pastoral and the pedagogic aspects of teaching, rather than with 'subject knowledge' can thus be excluded from claims to high status and to the generous resource allocation and higher scale posts which such status can bring. Thus subject-dominated perceptions of 'what counts' as high-status, professional expertise, coupled with the emphasis still given to the importance of examinations and 'academic' work, may well have contributed to the low and marginal position of remedial teachers and their pupils and to the concomitant lack of resources and policy attention.

As will be suggested in the next chapter, certain changes in secondary education may be encouraging a more important and central role for remedial education. It is possible therefore that the redefinition of remedial education will effect some change in traditional status. However that status remains a significant aspect of the context of such change. Firstly, dissatisfaction with the position accorded remedial education and remedial teachers may well have provided a particular impetus towards the development of approaches which could enhance the remedial teacher's role and status and the importance of remedial teaching and provision. Secondly, the traditional dominance of academic curricula within secondary education and of subject-based perceptions of professional status may well impinge on the possibilities of such enhancement and thus make necessary changes in the status of remedial education somewhat difficult to secure.

Thirdly, the legacies of traditional status may continue to influence the attitudes of both remedial and subject teachers. The low and marginal status of remedial education and of its teachers and their pupils is thus likely to be an important element in the redefinition of remedial education.

THE DIVERSITY OF REMEDIAL EDUCATION

Despite the unifying thread of a common concern with lack of educational progress, the diversity of policies and practices subsumed under the term 'remedial education' remains one of the most striking characteristics of this area of educational provision. Remedial education may be provided for pupils grouped in special classes or for pupils withdrawn from mainstream lessons for a number of periods each week. Such pupils may be selected on the basis of attainments in literacy or numeracy, on the results of intelligence tests or perhaps because they have 'social' as well as educational problems. Some schools may offer remedial tuition for pupils of every age group: others may limit it to pupils in the earlier years of secondary schooling. Other schools may offer few special arrangements, considering that courses provided for lower bands, streams or sets adequately comprise remedial provision. There may be a wide range of supporting services within an authority or there may be very few. Even remedial teachers themselves are a somewhat diverse group. The study carried out by Clunies-Ross and Wimhurst found that of the 800 specialist teachers of 'slow learners' questioned, a quarter had originally qualified as English teachers, a quarter had qualified in Humanities subjects, a sixth in mathematics or science, a sixth in creative or practical subjects and the remainder in a range of different subjects. This diversity of subject background was matched by a diversity of specialist training in the teaching of pupils with learning difficulties, ranging from attendance at a full-time course lasting a year to no specialist training at all (Clunies-Ross and Wimhurst,op.cit.pp.92-95).

There is also a great variety of terminology associated with remedial education. Pupils may be called 'remedial', 'slow learners', 'the less able', 'low achievers' or more recently, following the Warnock Report (DES,1978) and the 1981 Education Act, 'pupils with special educational needs'. Many

8

of these terms imply a particular cause of learning difficulties - that the pupil is slow to learn or has less ability than his/her peers. However such terms are often used interchangeably or without imputing a particular cause, so that no specific, semantic meaning can be assumed. Similarly, remedial departments may be called 'compensatory', 'opportunity', 'progress' or 'basic skills' departments without necessarily providing different forms of provision. Remedial teachers may also have a variety of names.

This diversity of terminology and provision is further compounded by a diversity of views about the aims, content and functions of remedial education. Commenting on the future of remedial education, Edwards (1983) has identified a number of issues about which there seems to be little common agreement. For example, there is the issue of the relationship between 'remedial', 'special' and 'ordinary' education. Various writers have put forward different conceptions of that relationship. Westwood (1975) has suggested that special education may be divided into four categories, of which remedial education is one. Brennan (1977) on the other hand, has argued that remedial education is that part of special education which takes place outside special schools, in other words it is not the content but the location of provision which distinguishes remedial education. Golby and Gulliver (1979) have identified a dichotomy between the provision made in full-time special classes for pupils seen to be of low intellectual ability and that made for pupils seen to merely need a period of temporary coaching before return to ordinary classes. They have suggested that the term 'remedial', which means 'rectifying' is most properly applied to the latter form of provision. Clark, though, has argued that it is 'too simplistic to talk in terms of special education for the dull and remedial education for the bright' (1976,p.5) not least because policies on eligibility for remedial help vary so much from area to area. Adoption of policies using the term 'special educational needs' for all forms of special provision, including remedial education, may overcome some of this confusion between special and remedial education: nevertheless a considerable diversity of practice and provision may remain.

Edwards (op.cit.) has also pointed out that there is a diversity of opinion about the focus of remedial teaching and about the expertise which the

remedial teacher should possess. He gives the
example that the constitutional components of
literacy difficulties have been stressed by some
writers (e.g. Tansley,1967), the emotional and
motivational aspects by others (e.g. Lawrence,1973).
Clark (op.cit.) has also highlighted the variety of
practices apparent within remedial education across
and within LEAs, as has Sampson (1975) in her study
of its historical development. Certainly the range
of techniques and materials employed in classrooms
does seem to vary considerably. The assessment of
learning difficulties, for example, may vary from
the use of a simple reading test to the deployment
of a sophisticated battery concerned with every
aspect of a pupil's capacities for learning. Work
on reading may involve the teaching of only the
basic decoding skills and strategies or a
considerable extension to facilitate the development
of 'higher order' skills such as inferential
comprehension. Techniques of reading instruction
may be based on very different theories of the
reading process (Miller,1981). Remedial help may be
concentrated on literacy skills alone, on literacy
and numeracy together, or in other instances, may be
closely related to problems with 'mainstream'
subjects. Given this range of policies and
curricular practices to be found within and across
LEAs, a range which is certainly apparent in the
surveys which have been carried out on remedial
provision (e.g. Brennan,1979, Clunies-Ross and
Wimhurst,1983, DES,1984, Hyde,1984) it does indeed
seem to be the case that as far as remedial
education is concerned, 'there are as many
definitions of the term as there are practitioners'
(Gains,1980,p.8).

Such diversity is significant to the context of
change for two reasons. Firstly it has given rise
to much concern about the need to provide clearer
aims and objectives for remedial education (e.g.
Clark,op.cit., McNicholas,1976, Gains,op.cit.) and
thus pull together the apparently fragmented nature
of provision. The ensuing debate engendered by
diversity has thus perhaps had some positive
ramifications in that remedial teachers have
continued to look for alternatives to the mix of
policies and practices traditionally found within
the field. Like the low and marginal status of
remedial provision, an apparently somewhat negative
feature has thus provided positive impetus towards
change. At the same time, such diversity may
continue to be problematic in respect to the

implementation of such change, since any redefinition, with its apparent unity of approach, may become fragmented at the level of the diverse policies and practices to be found in individual schools and LEAs. It is important therefore to try and establish whether diversity has been a consequence of a confusion or disagreement over aims and objectives, which might be resolved through new policies, or whether such diversity is more deeply embedded in the nature of remedial education and the context of secondary education, which may restrict the possibilities for change.

The variety of aims and objectives, policies and practices identified by Clark (op.cit.), McNicholas (op.cit.) and Gains (op.cit.), amongst others, as being a cause for concern, do seem frequently to be imputed to a lack of clarity in thinking. If this is indeed the case, then a clearly formulated redefinition of remedial education would offer opportunities to establish a more unified approach and pattern of accepted 'good practice'. It would also seem that a certain amount of confusion over aims and objectives could be attributed to the particular historical development of remedial education. For example, it could be suggested that in respect to the relationship between 'special' and 'ordinary' education, much of the debate which has taken place has been rooted in assumptions about the different needs of 'inherently dull' and of 'temporarily retarded' pupils, distinctions bequeathed by Burt (1937) and Schonell (1942). However, even when these distinctions were given more credence than they are now, remedial teachers still had to deal in practice with heterogeneous groups (Collins,1953, Cleugh,1957) and thus a lack of clarity in respect to the aims and objectives of remedial education was generated. The more flexible approach to remedial education now being mooted, in particular its incorporation into a wider definition of special education following the Warnock Report and the 1981 Education Act, may indeed resolve some past debates.

In addition though, it could be suggested that much of the diversity of remedial education is in part a consequence of the 'non-normative' nature of the category 'remedial pupil'. Looking at special education, Tomlinson has argued that

> the answer to the question 'what is' an ESN(M) child or a maladjusted child will depend more on the values, beliefs and interests of those

> making the judgement than on any qualities
> intrinsic to the child.
> (1982,p.66)

It could be argued that the category of 'remedial
pupil' (or other terms) is similarly open to a wide
variety of interpretations, which in turn are
dependent on a range of possibly conflicting values,
beliefs and interests. Thus it may not be possible
to 'scientifically' or 'objectively' define
universal criteria for assessing who is a 'remedial
pupil' or what is meant by 'remedial education',
with the consequence that policies and practices
will remain diverse. Moreover, categories of
pupils' needs and problems and decisions on
appropriate provision are further dependent on
particular school contexts, on factors such as the
organisation of the curriculum, the particular
perspectives of subject and remedial teachers,
grouping practices, pupil intake, resource
allocation and external demands and pressures.
Given the variety of such contexts, it would seem
almost impossible to provide universally accepted
models of 'good practice'. Certainly it cannot be
assumed that a greater clarity of aims and
objectives, or the shedding of confusing, historical
legacies of thought and practice, will necessarily
bring a unified approach to remedial education.
Diversity may well remain a significant feature of
the context of change, with a number of implications
for the implementation of a redefinition of remedial
education.

THE 'EXPERTISE' OF THE REMEDIAL TEACHER AND THE
'COMMUNITY' OF REMEDIAL EDUCATION

Although a diversity of policies and practices is
therefore a significant feature of remedial
education, there are some common threads which are
also important to the context of change. Firstly
those who work in the field, whatever their views on
appropriate approaches and techniques, do have a
common concern with learning difficulties and a
commitment to remediation. Secondly the remedial
teacher is often seen to have a particular
'expertise' which perhaps affords some sense of
communal identity and which delineates an area of
particular responsibilities within a school.
    Such expertise is often seen to include
knowledge of the causes and manifestations of

learning difficulties and of techniques for overcoming such problems. It may thus include knowledge of assessment procedures, teaching methods and materials and also knowledge of 'counselling' or other approaches to the behavioural or emotional problems which can be linked to learning failure. It could also be suggested that remedial teaching is often seen to involve a particular pedagogy, based primarily on individualised diagnosis and teaching, with remedial techniques being chosen to suit the strengths and problems of individual pupils. Such an individual pedagogy is not unique to remedial teaching, but given that the majority of teaching in schools tends to take place in large classes, where individualised work is not always the dominant pattern of instruction, this accentuation on individual help does seem to be a salient feature of perceived expertise and certainly has been used to justify withdrawal on an individual or small group basis. The approach of the remedial teacher can also perhaps be further distinguished by the emphasis often given to the affectual aspects of learning, in particular the consequences which learning difficulties may have for a pupil's personality, behaviour and self-esteem. All teachers may play a pastoral role of course but this aspect of a teacher's work may be particularly highlighted in remedial education, making the personal qualities of remedial teachers a part of the web of their expertise.

The expertise of the remedial teacher is particularly rooted in knowledge of child development and educational psychology and this knowledge, coupled with knowledge and experience of learning difficulties and their remediation, could be considered as the remedial teacher's 'subject', an equivalent to the knowledge of subjects such as history or biology held by teachers within a school. Thus the 'basic skills' of literacy and numeracy, which in their universality to all subjects would seem to negate any claim to special or particular knowledge are transformed into a special 'subject' through the particular expertise seen to be needed to teach such skills to pupils with learning difficulties. Such 'subject knowledge'[4], allied to a particular style of pedagogy and to responsibilities for pupils with learning difficulties, could be seen to sustain the identification of remedial teachers as a particular grouping within schools. In turn such groupings may be seen to have links not only between schools,

forged by common responsibilities and demands, but
with teacher training establishments, where similar
specialists offer training in remedial education,
with specialist advisers and more tenuously perhaps,
with colleagues working in special education or in
research activities concerned with learning
difficulties. Thus despite the diversity of
remedial education, it is possible to posit a
'community' of those involved in this particular
field, somewhat analogous to the subject groupings
or 'subject communities' centred around other
specialist areas of knowledge or subjects such as
mathematics, history, science and geography.

To view remedial education as being a community
of people with some common precepts and approaches
to particular problems is to bring another important
dimension to the context of change. As Ball has
commented in respect to other areas of the
curriculum, a 'subject' can then be viewed 'not as
an abstract intellectual conception but as a
changing body of knowledge produced by a social
collectivity' (1983,p.62). This offers
opportunities to examine how views of remedial
education have changed within the community of those
who work within the field, establish what
individuals and organisations have exerted an
influence on its development and analyse how
individuals and groups have interpreted and
implemented new knowledge and new approaches in
practice[5]. Change need not then be posed in terms
of fortuitous circumstances or discoveries or in
terms of the simple march of progress or indeed,
remain unexplored. Rather, credence can be given to
the importance of social action and interaction, to
the contribution of individuals and organisations
within the community and its wider social and
educational context. Some purchase on the complex
processes of change could then be gained.

Remedial education is not a subject in the
usual sense of the word, its precepts being allied
more to pedagogical practice than to an area of
knowledge which, amongst other things, is to be
transmitted to pupils. Perhaps therefore
'community' rather than 'subject community' might be
a more appropriate descriptive term. Nevertheless
links with studies of other subject communities
could well be made, drawing on the analyses recently
developed in this field by a number of sociologists
of education[6], to examine their relevance to
remedial education. Such work would also have the
additional benefit of possibly offsetting previous

sociological neglect of remedial education as an important and relevant field of enquiry.

So far it has been suggested that further study of the community of remedial education, of its common and typical precepts and of its segments and diversities could provide a useful analytical framework for examining what could be termed 'internal' change. In addition though, to characterise remedial education as one of the 'subject communities' within a school is also to suggest one means of analysing the new forms of social interaction presumed in the redefinition of remedial education which is the focus of this book. Some of this interaction, such as the sharing of the remedial teacher's expertise with subject teachers, to help them provide for pupils with learning difficulties in the mainstream curriculum, could perhaps be viewed as interaction between members of different communities, each with their own knowledge, pedagogy and perspectives. Such a conception could give access to the processes of defining and defending boundaries, negotiation and collaboration which such new 'partnerships' are likely to engender, and would also usefully locate remedial education within the complex web of academic and social relationships which make up the community of any school.

It may well be the case therefore that the expertise of remedial teaching, as perceived and as utilised in practice, in bringing together and sustaining a particular community of teachers may be a significant aspect of the context of change in that such a community can provide resources, a structure and participants for developing a redefinition of remedial education. Given too that such a community can provide a sense of communal identity, will define and defend its boundaries and suggest norms of 'good practice' for members, it may well influence both the content and the mode of change. The importance of community membership and identity and the influence of various segments of that community will thus be considered in later chapters. However the expertise of remedial teaching is not only important in this respect. Such expertise is also posited to have an important function in the redefinition of remedial education, for it is proposed that such expertise should be shared with the subject teacher in order to engender new approaches to remedial provision 'across the curriculum'. The components of that expertise, both perceived and actual, will thus be crucial to any change. In addition, such expertise may well have to be modified and developed to facilitate new ways of working. The relationship and the possible tensions between traditional and new expertise will also therefore be a part of the context of change. Finally, dissatisfaction with traditional expertise has contributed to the development of new apporoaches, thus again making expertise a significant aspect of the context of change. This dissatisfaction will now be more fully discussed.

THE END OF THE 'AMBULANCE SERVICE'?

Traditional remedial education has been criticised on a number of counts. There has been concern over the basic organisational framework in which remedial education has been provided, about some of the assumptions which underlie traditional approaches to remedial teaching and about the general effectiveness of remedial measures. This concern has thus focused on both the inadequacies of traditional expertise and on the manner in which it has been provided.

Traditional remedial education has been primarily concerned with the individual pupil. Research and classroom practice has centred on the causes of learning difficulties, on assessment procedures and on techniques for the remediation of discovered problems. The focus has thus been the 'deficits' within an individual, rather than the quality of his or her educational environment. In addition, as Golby and Gulliver (1979) have pointed out, such intervention has been based on implicit assumptions that there is a level of functioning which can be regarded as 'normal' and other levels which can then be viewed as 'abnormal'. Remedial education, concerned with these apparently 'abnormal', individual levels of functioning is thus based on an 'ideology of pathology'. In consequence, remedial teachers have come to view themselves as special 'therapists' concerned with the remediation of pathological deficits whilst other teachers tend to consider that such pupils are not their concern and are not part of their normal responsibilities.

Golby and Gulliver (ibid.) suggest that the 'ideology of pathology' arose largely because psychologists first showed an interest in individual differences. Although many benefits did accrue from this psychological work, it also buttressed an approach to mass education which viewed weakness as abnormality. The psychological approach, with its emphasis on psychometrics, also gave additional support to beliefs that ability could be measured and that pupils could consequently be grouped and taught accordingly, as in the tri-partite system which was established following the 1944 Education Act. Neither the assumptions about innate ability nor the consequent organisation of educational provision were questioned at first and instead, activity in remedial education was directed towards more sophisticated techniques for discovering the nature and extent of individual differences and difficulties and towards techniques for teaching pupils thus identified as being in some way 'deficient' or 'abnormal'.

This approach had a number of consequences for remedial education. Not least it meant that energy was directed towards changing individuals, with little regard being given to the possibility that school curricula or teaching methods were also possibly at fault. In the absence of change in these features of schools, the pupils referred to remedial teachers rarely dropped in number, even though individuals might improve their attainments in basic skills and be returned to the mainstream. Moreover since remedial pupils were often implicitly regarded as 'abnormal', remedial provision and its pupils were subject to the stigma of 'abnormality'. The emphasis given in schools to academic success and achievement further compounded such stigma and a low and marginal status was accorded to both remedial pupils and their teachers. Given that remedial teachers have thus been faced with the educational equivalent of the labours of Sisyphus, never overcoming the need for remedial help and have been accorded low status and few resources for the task, it is perhaps not surprising that there was increasing dissatisfaction about the organisation of remedial provision. This dissatisfaction was then further elaborated in the light of research which appeared to challenge the very validity of remedial measures.

Criticism of remedial measures in part focused on certain assumptions about identification and assessment, in particular the belief that abilities were innate and easily measured. The assumption that remedial education was concerned with 'putting right' certain deficits in basic skills so that pupils could fulfil their potential was increasingly questioned. The causes of learning difficulties were seen to be more complex and wide ranging than previously assumed and it was no longer accepted that ability could be easily measured in order to categorise pupils[7]. However the belief that pupils could perhaps be put into categories like 'retarded' or 'backward', on the lines advocated by Burt and Schonell, could probably have been changed in favour of more flexible definitions of learning difficulties, without radical changes in remedial education. Changes in knowledge, techniques and approaches are a constant feature of remedial education, with new methods and assessment techniques being adopted and old ones discarded as new research or ideas are mooted[8]. At the same time as this questioning took place however, the effectiveness of remedial education, as traditionally organised, was being queried in a way which suggested that new teaching methods alone were not the answer. The whole approach of withdrawing or separating pupils for extra help, outside the context of the mainstream curriculum, was being doubted.

Remedial education has always had its critics. Collins (1972) for example, described it as a 'hoax' and suggested that the maturation of pupils could be as effective as special remedial help. A series of research studies on the long-term benefits of remedial help also raised doubts about the effectiveness of remedial provision, particularly in the area of reading. Although, as Mosely has commented in summarising much of this research, it could be demonstrated that remedial help does result in some improvements in pupils' reading skills and without this help the immediate gains are very much less, the long-term results between pupils who did and did not receive such help often appeared to be the same (1975,p.125)[9]. The perceived need for long-term, 'follow-up' support and for changes in the teaching given to pupils with difficulties in mainstream classes suggested the desirability of a new approach. As the National Association for Remedial Education was to comment in its 1979 guidelines on the role of remedial teachers, the integration of remedial education into the general educational provision might help to offset the weaknesses identified by follow up research into the long-term effects of remedial education (NARE,1979). Moreover pupils might better acquire the literacy and other skills needed for learning subjects in the actual context of the subject lessons themselves, rather than through separate and unrelated tuition.

Given too that every area of the curriculum has potential for 'supporting and reinforcing basic skills' (Gains,1980,p.8), instead of preparing pupils, through special remedial help, for learning in subject lessons, it might be better to prepare the subject lessons in accordance with the learning needs of pupils. Thus the remedial teacher's expertise should be directed not just to remedying the deficits of individual pupils but towards content, materials and teaching methods across the curriculum. Such an approach might also begin to break down those features of the curriculum and of teaching and organisation which sometimes generated and certainly often exacerbated many of the learning difficulties experienced by pupils.

Thus the function and content of remedial education, the provision of an 'ambulance service' within schools was increasingly questioned. The 'ambulance service' was seen to have serious limitations. It concentrated on individuals, accentuated their deficits and 'treated' them as though they were 'abnormal' or 'sick'. In particular it prevented any consideration being given to the 'accident-prone' nature of the system which was generating such casualties (Golby and Gulliver,op.cit.). Given too that the quality of the 'first aid' which was provided was somewhat open to doubt, it was crucial to find a new role and direction for remedial education and for remedial teachers. The prevention of learning difficulties, through appropriate curricula and teaching methods, the provision of adequate resources and the development of effective screening and monitoring procedures should be the new focus of remedial work. As Golby and Gulliver (ibid.) aptly put it, the remedial teacher should be less of an 'ambulance man' and become more a 'consultant on road safety'.

Whether such a new role can be established and the limitations of traditional policies and practice be overcome is another question. The traditional tenets and assumptions of remedial work may continue to influence both the mode and the implementation of a redefined remedial education. Certainly though, dissatisfaction with traditional practice has provided some of the impetus towards the development of a new approach and towards demands for a new direction and content for the remedial teacher's expertise. The expertise and the practices of remedial education are thus very much part of the context of change.

19

CONCLUSION

It has now been suggested that there are a number of elements to the context of changes in remedial education. This chapter has particularly looked at those issues which have perhaps been the prime foci of concern from members of the community of remedial education. The issues of expertise, of status, of diversity and of traditional practice need of course to be put in a wider context. As will be suggested in the next chapter, a number of changes in secondary education may have forced remedial education to take a new role. It is not only the limitations of traditional remedial education which have provided an impetus towards change, although perceptions of particular problems in traditional policies and practice may well have shaped the direction and substance of redefinition. Equally the implementation of any redefinition of remedial education will be dependent not only in changes in the views and practice of remedial teachers themselves but on the views and practices of the subject teachers involved and will be influenced by the particular features of schools in which innovation takes place and by more general developments in education. However in beginning to unpack some of the salient features of the context of redefinition, such innovation and change can be seen as more than a chance development, the features of which are just dependent on new knowledge or new ideas. Instead, it becomes possible to delineate some of the many issues, processes and changes which may be involved. Before these are considered in more detail however, the substance, history and context of the redefinition of remedial education will be examined.

NOTES

1. The term 'redefinition' will be used to describe this new approach to remedial education because it suggests an active process of change and moots the possibility of comparison with other studies of the redefinition of subjects (see Note 5).
2. At the time of writing it was being proposed that the name of NARE be changed to National Association for Special Educational Needs (NASEN). However since during the period of redefinition discussed in this book, the name of the

association was NARE and all its publications discussed were published under this name, the name NARE will be used to avoid any possible confusion.

3. Estimates of the incidence of pupils with learning difficulties within the school population do vary but figures of around 15% have been commonly mooted, with the Warnock Report (DES,1978) suggesting that some 20% of pupils may have 'special educational needs' (though not all of these 'needs', of course, involve the learning difficulties which have traditionally been the responsibility of remedial teachers).

4. Such 'subject knowledge' could be usefully analysed to delineate in more detail what precisely is considered to be the remedial teacher's 'expertise' and given the diversity of remedial practices, further research would also be needed to establish the extent to which 'expertise' is commonly defined within the community of remedial education. The various texts on learning difficulties/remedial education/slow learners (e.g. Bell,1970, Leach and Raybould,1977, Westwood,1975) could provide a useful starting point, as examples and summaries of knowledge and expertise required of remedial teachers.

5. Use could well be made of other studies of subject communities and subject redefinition (e.g. Ball,1982, Ball,1983, Ball and Lacey,1980, Cooper,1982,1985, Goodson,1983, Goodson and Ball,1984), examining the pertinence of their models, analysis and findings to the redefinition of remedial education.

6. See Note 5.

7. The DES Survey of 'slow learners' in secondary schools in 1971, for example, took a much wider definition of such pupils, to include factors other than 'limited ability' and suggested that 'social handicaps' could depress intellectual potential.

8. Richmond (1985) gives some examples of such changes, in relation to the assessment and remediation of reading difficulties, which illustrate the way in which remedial methods are constantly altering.

9. Such studies, such as Lovell, Byrne and Richardson (1963) may or may not have been correct - the effectiveness of remedial measures is still being debated. However their influence was important (e.g. NARE,1979).

Chapter Two

THE REDEFINITION OF REMEDIAL EDUCATION

The 'new approach' to remedial education which has
been mooted in the past decade or so involves a
number of changes in traditional policies and
practice. For example, it has been suggested that
the aims of remedial education should be more
closely linked to those of mainstream education
(McNicholas,1976, Gains,1980) and that the remedial
teacher should develop a 'new partnership' with
subject teachers in order to develop 'remedial work
across the curriculum' (Gulliford,1979,
Gains,op.cit.). The National Association for
Remedial Education (NARE) has argued for an extended
role for remedial teachers, to involve not only
traditional responsibilities such as the assessment
and teaching of pupils with learning difficulties
but also the provision of advice and help for
subject teachers and work alongside the subject
teacher in the mainstream classroom. Remedial
teachers should also develop new strategies and
procedures for identifying, assessing and monitoring
pupils with learning difficulties within a school,
facilitate close cooperation with other agencies and
promote the development of 'whole school policies'
for remedial work and special educational needs
(NARE,1979,1985). A new 'preventive' import to
remedial education is thus being suggested, with the
emphasis now being put on changing the
organisational and curricular context of learning
difficulties through the dissemination of the
remedial teacher's expertise and through the
development of explicit, 'whole school policies' for
pupils with learning difficulties. In addition, the
emphasis now given to collaborative work between
remedial and subject teacher, to support for pupils
within the mainstream classroom and to development
of the subject teacher's expertise on learning

22

difficulties, also posits a greater integration of both remedial teachers and their pupils within the mainstream of school life, in contrast to the isolation and marginality which have traditionally been features of remedial education.

THE DEVELOPMENT OF A REDEFINITION

This new approach or redefinition of remedial education has been supported and developed by the National Association for Remedial Education (NARE). In addition, individual members of NARE and other teachers and teacher trainers in the field of remedial education have provided a number of accounts of new approaches and developments which have contributed to the process of redefinition. One of the first to suggest the need for change was Ian Galletley, who described how remedial teachers might 'do away' with themselves by educating their colleagues to deal with pupils with learning difficulties in mixed ability classes. His 'opportunities department' also abolished permanent withdrawal of pupils for remedial help, substituting short courses for all who might need them when appropriate (Galletley,1976). A similar approach was developed at Countesthorpe College in Leicestershire, where it was decided that the remedial department should work more closely with other colleagues, withdrawing some pupils for extra help but also giving support in mixed ability classes and providing suitably modified materials. Later, remedial teachers were attached to the teams of teachers responsible for a particular year group and provided support and withdrawal in that context, sharing their expertise during planning and through informal courses for staff (Chisholm,1977).

The potential of such new approaches was also being considered by members of NARE. At a conference appropriately entitled 'Remedial Education at the Crossroads', in 1975, Paul Widlake, the then President, made his call for a new direction in which remedial teachers would emerge from their hidden isolation, in cloakrooms and under stages, to take their rightful place alongside other colleagues. Remedial education had to be recognised as being as important as other areas of teaching and should be placed 'squarely within the normal educational process' (Widlake,1975,pp.106-7). Such sentiments were echoed by Clark, at the same conference, who pointed out that

> remedial education has perhaps in the past been
> guilty of too little attempt to coordinate
> specialist teaching with the ongoing work of
> the classroom to which the child must return
> ... [this] necessitates a broadening of the
> conception of remedial education
> (1976,p.7)

and by McNicholas (1976) who considered that the
aims of remedial education should be viewed in the
context of the general aims of education. Moreover,
McNicholas suggested, there should be a greater
concern with preventive measures and thus

> always broadening its scope, permeating and
> integrating with the main stream of education,
> remedial education should seek as one of its
> ultimate aims the eventual phasing out of
> remediation in schools.
> (ibid.,p.115)

Two years later, at a further conference of
NARE with the theme of 'Guidelines for the Future',
Gulliford (1979) proposed the notion of 'remedial
work across the curriculum' as a slogan for future
years, in order to develop a wider conception of
provision. He also suggested that the subject
teacher should be encouraged to take more
responsibility for pupils with learning
difficulties, aided and advised by remedial teachers
in partnership. In turn, remedial teachers should
become more familiar with curricular issues and with
'methods of organising and managing the range of
alternatives of remedial help' (ibid.,p.149). At
the same conference, McNicholas developed the idea
of the remedial teacher as a 'change agent',
concerned with strategies for innovation
(McNicholas,1979) and Evans (1979) stressed the need
to emphasise 'prevention' rather than remediation.
The idea of providing 'remedial education
across the curriculum' was then later developed by
Gains. Looking at the prospects for remedial
education in the 1980s, he emphasised the importance
of early 'preventive' work and also suggested that
remedial teachers should indeed develop new
'partnerships' with subject and class teachers in
which

> the specialist remedial teacher should be in
> the business of giving away his or her skills,
> at the same time being aware of the potential

every area of the curriculum has for supporting and reinforcing basic skills.
(1980,p.8)

Moreover such 'partnerships' should be combined with greater involvement in school organisation and management, to facilitate the development of comprehensive strategies for pupils with learning difficulties.

Further articles in the journal of NARE, Remedial Education (now called Support for Learning)[1] have since further developed a number of these ideas. Lewis (1984), for example, has argued the benefits of developing the subject teacher's expertise and responsibilities for pupils with learning difficulties through collaboration between remedial and subject teacher. Remedial or 'support' teachers, as he terms them, should be involved with the adaptation of curricular materials and should encourage subject teachers to experiment with their own classroom management and organisation, drawing on the group and individual programmes used in remedial education. Daniels (1984) also considers that becoming involved with team teaching and helping with the planning of courses in subject areas are important dimensions of the remedial teacher's role. Moreover, it is important that pupils with learning difficulties should be able to follow the common curriculum and although withdrawal arrangements may be made for certain pupils, remedial (or 'supportive education') teachers should not be organised in a separate department, working in isolation, but be members of a team cooperating with all teachers within a school. To complement such arguments, there have also been a number of articles in the NARE journal which have looked at learning difficulties in subjects such as science, history and geography as well as the more traditional concerns of literacy and numeracy, and editorial support has also been given to collaborative, cross-curricular work.

The sharing of expertise in a new advisory role has also been supported by other writers, such as Sewell (1982), who argues that the main aim of the remedial teacher or 'coordinator of special education' should be to ensure that pupils with learning difficulties are taught 'in stimulating and appropriate ways across the curriculum' (p.59). Where this does not occur, Sewell suggests that the coordinator should intervene in a number of ways. Capable and sympathetic staff should be trained in the teaching of reading. Staff sensitivity towards the linguistic demands made in subject lessons should be developed, possibly through the medium of an 'English Across the Curriculum' Group. Work should be undertaken in mathematics and other subject areas to foster the professional development of teachers in their own disciplines, with certain teachers taking responsibility in their own subject area for the development of courses and materials, under the coordination of the teacher in charge of special provision. This coordinator should also be responsible for developing relationships with the community and outside agencies.

Such accounts[2] illustrate the many dimensions of the redefinition of remedial education which is now being put forward by a number of practitioners and by NARE. Traditional responsibilities for assessment and withdrawal are to be combined with collaborative work with subject teachers to provide help across the curriculum for pupils with learning difficulties. The former isolation of both remedial teachers and their pupils is to be replaced with a greater integration in mainstream classes and subjects, within the context of a 'whole school', cross-curricular approach to remedial work. In addition, through the sharing of expertise, the remedial teacher will effect changes in curricula, pedagogy and organisation.

The models developed by individual writers and by NARE are not identical. There are differences of emphasis and approach in respect to the focus and the organisation of remedial work. As will be discussed later in this chapter, one problematic aspect of the redefinition of remedial education concerns the somewhat diverse way in which it has been elaborated and the lack of specific, detailed prescription of changes in curricula, methodology and the remedial teacher's role. Nevertheless it is possible, and indeed it is important, to identify some common threads of this suggested redefinition and thus begin to understand its substance. Those common threads or themes will therefore now be discussed.

THE SUBSTANCE OF THE REDEFINITION

Five major themes of change can perhaps be discerned, each having a number of implications for traditional policies and practice. Firstly there is the question of changes in the clientele of remedial education. Remedial education has traditionally been concerned with the provision of special curricula for pupils seen to have more permanent learning problems and also with the provision of some additional help for pupils seen to have more temporary difficulties. Such distinctions, the legacy of Burt and Schonell, were not however always maintained in practice and remedial teachers often found themselves involved with a variety of pupil needs in a climate of thinking which increasingly challenged the plausibility of such distinctions. The need for flexibility in any definition of learning difficulties was thus recognised by the National Association for Remedial Education, when it suggested that remedial education should be concerned with

> the prevention, investigation and treatment of learning difficulties from whatever source they emanate and which hinder the normal educational development of the student.
> (NARE, 1977)

Such a definition not only avoided making distinctions between pupils on the grounds of their imputed ability but also included the effective and social, as well as the cognitive, dimensions of learning difficulties. It thus offered a broad base for the definition of the remedial teacher's potential clientele and, as was later noted by NARE, in its guidelines on the role of remedial teachers, also released remedial teachers from being concerned only with difficulties in the basic subjects (NARE, 1979). Concerned with the prevention as well as with the remediation of learning difficulties from a broad range of sources, remedial teachers could then legitimately work across the curriculum as well as fulfilling more traditional responsibilities. This more flexible and wide-ranging definition of clientele is thus an important theme of redefinition.

Provision for this wide range of potential clients is to be developed in a different context as well, and one which is somewhat different from that of traditional remedial education. 'Withdrawal' groups or special classes have often been provided in isolation from the mainstream school. Although the redefinition of remedial education does not preclude some withdrawal or even the deployment of special classes, it posits a major focus on support for pupils with learning difficulties within the mainstream class. The major context for remedial education is thus defined as the mainstream curriculum and the mainstream pupil groupings of the school. Such a new context also suggests that there will be a different content for remedial work. Remedial education has traditionally been concerned with the basic skills of literacy and numeracy. Such basic skills may now be developed through mainstream curricular materials and the content of remedial work be thus increasingly drawn from different subjects within the mainstream curriculum. Remedial teachers may also share their expertise with subject teachers. Some of the content of remedial work may thus be directed towards the pedagogy of the subject teacher, towards improving teaching methods or appropriate adaptation of learning resources.

This broader involvement in the organisation and curriculum of the mainstream of the school implies a change, too, in the expertise of the remedial teacher. Traditionally, such expertise has resided in the remedial teacher's capacity to make accurate diagnoses of learning difficulties and then provide appropriate remedial techniques. This expertise was thus primarily directed towards pupils, with a particular emphasis on instruction in basic skills. It is now being suggested that such 'diagnostic skills' should be extended to assess and 'remediate' the curriculum and organisation of a school, to facilitate improved provision for pupils with learning difficulties across the curriculum. New forms of expertise may thus be needed, such as a greater knowledge of individual subject content and method, of curriculum development, of the preparation of instructional materials and of teaching methods for different forms of pupils grouping. Such requirements have indeed been recognised by NARE, in its Guidelines on in-service education for remedial teachers (NARE,1982). It could also be argued that remedial teachers may need new inter-personal skills, for successful teacher-teacher interaction, to supplement those skills and attributes often seen to be necessary for successful teaching with pupils with learning difficulties (NARE,ibid., Smith,1982). In addition, a greater involvement in the development of 'whole school policies' would seem to require new organisational and management skills. Certainly there would seem to be some major changes needed in the traditional expertise of remedial teachers, and a concomitant revision of training (Gains,1985).

The redefinition of remedial education, therefore, posits a redefinition of the clientele, the context, the content and the expertise of remedial education. In addition, these changes are to be facilitated and brought together in what is perhaps the most important and central theme of redefinition, the redefinition of the remedial teacher's role. As noted earlier, there have been many arguments in favour of the extension of the remedial teacher's role from traditional responsibilities for assessment and tuition of pupils with learning difficulties to taking part in advisory and support work across the curriculum. The remedial teacher is also to play a more important management role, coordinating provision, encouraging staff training and developing 'whole school policies'. These new responsibilities will facilitate change in the context and content of remedial provision by legitimating the remedial teacher's involvement in the whole curriculum and the overall management of the school, and this wider involvement will in turn facilitate the remedial teacher's concern with a broad and flexible range of pupils and generate the need for new expertise. The redefinition of the role and responsibilities of the remedial teacher is thus a crucial component of the substance of the redefinition of remedial education.

The redefinition of remedial education is to be realised in a number of ways. A prerequisite to implementation is of course the recognition of this wider brief for the remedial teacher. Two other important means of realisation involve the initiation of a 'new partnership' between remedial and subject teacher and the development of 'whole school policies'[3]. The 'partnership' facilitates the sharing of the remedial teacher's expertise with the subject teacher, through consultation, the giving of advice and collaborative work on appropriate teaching materials and methods for pupils with learning difficulties. It may also encompass some form of team teaching, with the remedial teacher working alongside the subject teacher in the mainstream classroom, giving help and support to pupils with learning difficulties. 'Whole school policies' will be used to ensure that provision for such pupils is carefully planned across the curriculum and that responsibility for teaching them is not seen to be just that of the remedial teacher. Rather, through collaborative work and through agreement on strategies, organisation and provision, the teaching of pupils with learning difficulties will be seen as a 'whole school' question, a central part of the curriculum and organisation of the school.

Nevertheless it is not entirely clear how such 'partnerships' and policies, or indeed the new role of the remedial teacher, will develop in practice. The notions of 'partnership' and collaboration seem to suggest that remedial and subject teachers will have an equal and joint say in, and responsibility for, approaches to pupils with learning difficulties. However the notion of 'partnership' raises a whole number of issues about the relationship between remedial and subject teacher, including the issue of comparative status, who has the ultimate responsibility and indeed power to decide on how pupils shall be taught in subject lessons, whether in practice agreement can be reached between teachers who may have very different views on subject content and pedagogy and what implications there may be in terms of teachers' professional autonomy. Such issues have rarely been discussed. Rather it has often been assumed that given the benefits of this new approach for pupils and the improvements which are offered in terms of a more effective and appropriate provision, redefinition will be accepted. Remedial teachers may have to walk a 'diplomatic tightrope' in developing this new supportive, advisory and management role perhaps, but

> if what they offer is relevant and practical, they will quickly win the confidence of their colleagues. The remedial department, if used with imagination within the school, can affect attitudes and influence policy. It can make an impact on existing school organisation, curriculum development and allocation of resources.
> (Lewis, 1984, p. 11)

However, as will be discussed later, it does not appear that the redefinition of remedial education has as yet been widely implemented in schools. This may be due to a number of factors, but, as will be argued later in this book, the problems of implementation, including the problems of professional autonomy and of potential conflict within the 'partnership' of remedial and subject teacher, ought to be more widely and carefully considered. Certainly what is meant by support and advisory work, and by the 'partnership' between remedial and subject teacher, needs to be more closely defined.

The issues involved in the development of 'whole school policies' have also not received particularly detailed consideration. The remedial teacher may well make an important contribution to such policies, suggesting perhaps what forms of organisation and provision for pupils with learning difficulties should be established, what assessment procedures, how collaborative work between subject teacher and remedial teacher could be developed and what should be the substance of such collaboration. The remedial teacher may also have a number of ideas about teaching materials and methods, about the distribution of time and remedial staffing to different responsibilities and about ways in which decisions on policies should be made. At the same time,'whole school policies' need agreement and support from the whole staff. Are indeed the questions just outlined properly matters for a 'whole school policy' and if so can agreement be reached? As Boyd has commented, looking at the notion of 'whole school policies' in general, the issue is very much

> how one achieves the aim of persuading a school staff, made up of subject specialists with boundary maintenance a high priority, of 'restricted' and 'extended' professionals, of people with fundamentally different values, and indeed different ideas of the aim of education, to work together to produce effective whole school policies.
> (1985,p.80)

Nor does it seem to be entirely clear as to what such agreement should comprise. Is such a policy merely a statement of aims and objectives or should it consist of detailed agreement on staffing, organisation, curriculum and teaching methods? And how should it be decided and executed? Should it merely legitimate certain methods of working and then allow the 'detail' to be implemented by individual staff in their lessons or should it give detailed prescription as to the staffing, resources and methods of collaboration, teaching and organisation to be deployed?

The resolution of such questions may be considered to be a matter for individual schools. But at the same time they do have a general importance in terms of analysing what constitutes the redefinition of remedial education. Moreover, further discussion could offer better guidance to those teachers concerned to develop a new approach. A clearer conception of the 'partnership' and of 'whole school policies' might also begin to overcome some of the diversity of policies and practice endemic to remedial education, a diversity which has given rise to confusion about the aims of remedial education, and to concern about the inequalities of provision within and across LEAs. It would seem therefore that more attention should be given to these aspects of the redefinition of remedial education.

Equally, more consideration needs to be given to what constitutes the remedial teacher's role. The responsibilities involved in the new role of remedial teachers have been widely discussed and have been cogently summarised by NARE (1979,1985) to include teaching, support and advisory work, prescription on learning programmes and identification and assessment of pupils with learning difficulties. Teachers with overall responsibility for remedial work, heads of remedial or 'special needs support' departments, should also play a fuller management role, coordinating provision and developing policies. Remedial staff are therefore to be, variously, teachers, advisers, managers, 'partners', coordinators and 'change agents'. What is less clear is how much time and resources should be devoted to each aspect of a remedial teacher's responsibilities and what primarily should be their major role in schools. Again this could be considered to be a matter for the individual teacher and school, and yet to more clearly understand the substance of redefinition, to provide guidance and lessen diversity, it would seem important to decide whether most time should be spent on teaching or on advising and collaboration with subject teachers and more clearly delineate whether the remedial teacher is for example, a strong initiator of change or primarily a resource of knowledge and experience when change is desired by other colleagues. Otherwise a diversity of policies and practice, and quite possibly some confusion and even conflict could arise both within schools and within the community of remedial education.

Thus although it is possible to delineate the direction and the general substance of the redefinition of remedial education, many issues have not been completely resolved, in terms of detail and

actual practice. The redefinition of remedial
education involves the construction of a new
interface between remedial and mainstream education
but some of the bricks, and certainly the mortar, of
that construction have not yet been put into place.
However before some further aspects of this current
stage of redefinition are considered, it is
important to look at another issue, namely the
development of new approaches to 'special
educational needs'.

NEW APPROACHES TO 'SPECIAL EDUCATIONAL NEEDS'

This interface between remedial and mainstream
education has now been further developed to take
account of new approaches to the wider question of
'special educational needs'. The Warnock Report
(DES,1978) which gave rise to these new approaches,
crystallised increasing concern about the need to
modify certain features of special educational
provision. The Report proposed a new concept of
special education which would avoid categorisation
of pupils and schools and which would encompass
pupils in both ordinary and special schools. It
stated that

> our concept of special education is thus
> broader than the traditional one of education
> by special methods appropriate for particular
> categories of children. It extends beyond the
> idea of education provided in special schools,
> classes or units for children with particular
> types of disability and embraces the notion of
> any form of additional help, wherever it is
> provided, from birth to maturity, to overcome
> educational difficulties.
> (Para.1.10)

This broad definition would therefore
encompass the pupils who had been receiving remedial
education. Indeed later in the Report it was
suggested that 'a meaningful distinction between
remedial and special education can no longer be
maintained' (Para.3.39). Remedial education should
thus be absorbed under the wider umbrella of special
education.
This wide concept of special education was
incorporated into the 1981 Education Act. In this
Act a child is seen to have 'special educational
needs' if 'he has a learning difficulty which

requires special educational provision to be made to
meet those needs' (Section One). 'Learning
difficulty' is to include any form of difficulty
which is 'significantly greater than that of the
majority of children of the same age' (ibid.). The
DES Circulars which have accompanied the Act have
endorsed the Warnock Report's estimate that some 20
per cent of pupils within the whole school
population might have 'special educational needs'.
It seems clear therefore that 'remedial pupils' come
within this remit and should now be termed 'pupils
with special educational needs'.

The use of such new terminology is now becoming
more widespread. Sewell (1982) for example, has
suggested that the teacher in charge of remedial
provision should be termed the 'coordinator of
special education' and Daniels (1984) has also
commented on the need for a more appropriate term
such as 'special educational provision', instead of
'remedial education'. The National Association for
Remedial Education (which has proposed the adoption
of the new name of National Association for Special
Educational Needs) refers to a wider concept of
'special educational need' in its more recent
guidelines on in-service training and teaching roles
(NARE,1982,1985). The guidelines on 'Teaching Roles
for Special Educational Needs' (NARE,1985) suggest
that responsibility for the needs of children with
learning difficulties should be led by a 'special
educational needs coordinator', who should fulfil a
number of roles, including assessment, prescription,
teaching and pastoral work, support, liaison,
management and staff development. Such a
coordinator would be assisted by other 'special
educational needs support teachers'. Former
'remedial departments' would be called 'special
needs support departments'[4]. Such terms may well be
increasingly used in schools in future instead of
'remedial'.

However it is not just a question of changes in
terminology. Indeed it could be suggested that the
'special needs' approach represents a further
modification or redefinition of remedial education.
As noted earlier in Chapter One, remedial education
has always been somewhat invidiously juxtaposed
between special and ordinary education. If remedial
education is brought under the wider umbrella of
special educational provision, then this will
legitimate the abolition of formal distinctions
between 'remedial', 'special' and 'ordinary'
education and possibly, distinctions between pupils

with the types of learning difficulties which have traditionally been the remedial teacher's concern and pupils with other forms of special educational need, such as physical handicap or sensory impairment.

The new guidelines on teaching roles published by NARE (op.cit.) do not seem to be entirely clear about the possible delineation of responsibilities for special educational needs. The focus of these guidelines appears to be 'learning difficulties'. At the same time it is also suggested that the 'special educational needs coordinator' might support colleagues 'with ideas and techniques for the whole range of children with special educational needs' (p.8). Such a coordinator would also be involved with the identification of 'children with special needs' and with 'coordination of response to special educational needs', as part of a senior management team (ibid.,pp.8-9). These suggestions would seem to imply an expansion of the remedial teacher's former responsibilities to encompass pupils with all forms of 'special educational needs'. Indeed, given that the concept of 'special educational need' was developed to avoid rigid and discrete categorisation of pupils according to particular difficulties and handicaps, it would seem to be inappropriate to try and delineate a specific client group of pupils who are the responsibility of 'remedial' special needs teachers, with other pupils then being seen as the responsibility of different special needs teachers. Even if there was, for example, a specialised teacher of pupils with hearing impairments within a school, such teaching would have to be coordinated within the wider range of provision for pupils with special needs, with someone responsible for that overall coordination. Is that person then going to be a former head of the remedial department, a member of the school management staff or the specialist teacher? Some remedial teachers might be willing to take on the wider responsibilities implied in the term 'special educational needs coordinator': others might prefer to limit their brief, concerned that they might not have the range of knowledge and expertise required to coordinate or support provision for pupils across the range of 'special educational needs'. On the other hand, whatever the views of remedial teachers, particularly if the integration of pupils now in special schools is increased, such expertise may well have to be extended since remedial teachers may be seen as the professionals to whom such responsibilities should be given. Not every school will necessarily have a range of specialist teachers trained to work with pupils with a variety of handicaps and learning problems. Adoption of the term 'special needs teacher' for 'remedial teacher' may well generate expectations that such teachers will be responsible for all 'special educational needs' within a school, whatever their expertise or previous responsibilities[5].

As yet it is difficult to predict the outcome of changes in approach to special educational provision. Moreover, as with the implementation of new approaches to remedial provision, not all schools have as yet adopted the terminology nor the concept of 'special educational need' for pupils receiving remedial help. Nor has remedial education been universally integrated with other forms of special educational provision. The Warnock Report and the 1981 Education Act were welcomed by many practitioners in the field of remedial education, not least because of the recognition given to special educational needs in ordinary schools, and the recommendations of the Report and the implications of the ensuing legislation have been widely considered. However the consequences of such legislation and of any implementation of new approaches to special educational provision for the redefinition of remedial education cannot as yet be fully considered.

EXPLAINING REDEFINITION:
STRUCTURAL AND INTERACTIONAL ASPECTS OF CHANGE

There would seem to be a number of benefits which may accrue to pupils from the redefinition of remedial education. Such perceived benefits have provided many of the rationales for developing and implementing a new approach. For example it has been suggested that pupils with learning difficulties may be less stigmatised since they will not be withdrawn so frequently for remedial help but may receive such help alongside their peers in ordinary classrooms. Such pupils will also have access to the same learning experiences as their peers and to the specialist expertise of the subject teacher. The support and advice of the remedial teacher should ensure that such subject teaching is appropriately geared to the needs of such pupils and the development of 'whole-school policies' should ensure adequate planning and resource allocation. A broad and flexible definition of learning difficulties or 'special educational need' should avoid the problems engendered by rigid categorisation. Where the mainstream curriculum is used as a vehicle for overcoming learning difficulties and remedial help developed in the ordinary classroom, this may increase the effectiveness of remedial work. Such support may also be of benefit to the subject teacher, developing expertise and affording more time and attention to be given to pupils within the class[6]. It is perhaps rather surprising therefore that given such apparent benefits, this approach has only been mooted quite recently and was not instituted when remedial education first developed following the expansion of secondary education with the 1944 Education Act. Perhaps it is simply a question of the 'march of progress' or of missed opportunities to change ideas and organisation.

However change does not take place in a vacuum, rather it has to be examined in relation to the overall context of secondary schooling and pedagogical practice. Changes in attitudes and ideas have to be related to such social and educational contexts. For example, the context in which remedial education developed following the 1944 Education Act was not particularly conducive to any development of an integrated, cross-curricular approach. As Golby and Gulliver (1979) have commented, the education service at that time needed an 'ambulance service' type of remedial education, based as it was on subject-oriented teaching, requiring competence in basic skills, in tightly streamed schools. Moreover the system was founded on notions of disparate pupil ability and a belief that pupils of differing abilities and aptitudes should be taught in discrete, homogenous units and be given different curricula. It would thus have been extremely difficult to establish a more integrated form of remedial education, particularly since remedial teachers also supported the idea that there were (usually innate) differences between children which necessitated special, separate provision.

As Golby and Gulliver (ibid.) have suggested, a number of more recent changes in secondary education have since forced remedial education to adopt a new role. The change to mixed ability grouping, for example, has entailed teachers paying more attention to the literacy demands made on pupils. The moves towards a common curriculum have led to some questioning of the value of extraction for remedial help since such extraction can exclude certain pupils from participation in the whole of the common curriculum. It may also be the case that the development of integrated studies has contributed to the breaking down of subject barriers so that teachers accept the value of collaborative work between departments. Such integration may also have made teachers less demanding in respect to what levels of literacy pupils should achieve, since conceptions of themselves and their subject may have altered. Thus the need for basic coaching in literacy (or numeracy), and thus for segregation of pupils with learning difficulties, may have diminished, with teachers being more willing to integrate such pupils and perhaps share responsibilities and expertise with remedial teachers.

New knowledge about learning difficulties may also be important. In particular, the efficacy of mental testing, and therefore the legitimacy of making formal distinctions between pupils on the grounds of low intellectual ability, has been challenged. It is also being increasingly recognised that reading and other basic skills are best learned in context and that separate remedial tuition may be neither effective nor beneficial. Indeed the ineffectiveness of some remedial measures, often ascribed particularly to lack of 'follow up' in mainstream classes, may have provided a particular impetus towards change[7]. In addition, within special and remedial education there has been a move away from medical or categorative models of learning difficulties and a new emphasis upon the educational aspects of handicap and the importance of the learning environment[8]. Research within the sociology of education, which stresses the importance of considering the context and processes of schooling rather than individual 'deficits' of pupils, may have provided further rationales for working on changes in curricula and organisation rather than just remedying the problems of individual pupils, rationales which may have been further strengthened by the growth of interest in the effectiveness of schools[9].

It could also be suggested that the pedagogical perspectives of teachers in secondary schools have changed to some degree, to facilitate and perhaps even create a demand for a different sort of remedial provision. Traditionally, such perspectives have been dominated by what Esland

(1971) has termed the 'psychometric' perspective, which conceives the child as an 'empty vessel' to be filled up with approved knowledge. In contrast, the 'epistemological' (or 'phenomenological') perspective stresses the interaction between the learner and his environment (Esland,ibid.). Crudely these two perspectives could be represented by the tenets of progressive primary school education, with its emphasis on experiential learning (the 'phenomenological' perspective) and by the pedagogical practices of most secondary schools, with their emphasis on the didactic transmission of established knowledge (the 'psychometric' perspective). The experiential approach, which focuses on 'process' rather than 'product', is however beginning to penetrate the secondary school, at least at the level of rhetoric and this development may be providing an encouraging context for the insertion of remedial teachers' expertise on learning processes and individual development[10]. Moreover, the development of a pedagogy appropriate to such processual learning and to mixed ability grouping, namely individual or resource-based learning, may also be encouraging the development of remedial work in mainstream classes. Such modes of organising learning can obviate the need for extraction, since work can be geared to individual levels of knowledge and skills. They are also appropriate for the flexible insertion of support from remedial teachers.

Finally, there are some wider social and educational issues which may have influenced the development of new approaches to remedial education. One such issue is that of equality. Although meritocratic models of comprehensive schooling may be dominant within secondary education (Ball,1984), with the 'grammar school curriculum' still powerfully pervasive (Hargreaves,1982), egalitarianism and the provision of opportunities for all pupils remain important issues. It can be argued that to develop comprehensive education because selection on the grounds of 'ability' is undesirable, but still retain selection and segregation on the grounds of 'disability', is a major contradiction. Thus pupils with learning difficulties in comprehensive schools (and for that matter, pupils in special schools) should be more fully integrated. To extract pupils for special help also undermines the 'social mix' that comprehensives are seen to offer. Such arguments may well have encouraged the development of a more integrated form of remedial provision and provided yet further rationales for its implementation[11].

Thus remedial education may well have changed as a consequence of these developments in secondary education. At the same time it is also important to recognise the role played by members of the community of remedial education, the 'interactional' element of subject redefinition[12], recognising in particular perhaps the influence of the National Association for Remedial Education. NARE has put forward various definitions of remedial education and has published guidelines on the role of remedial teachers, on in-service training, on the preparation of materials for 'remedial work across the curriculum' and on new approaches to 'special educational needs'. In addition, links have been established with other subject associations, to discuss collaborative work, materials and approaches towards remedial education and subject teaching. A number of remedial teachers and teacher educators concerned with training in the field of remedial education have written about new approaches to remedial provision in the journal of NARE, Remedial Education[13] and NARE conferences have discussed many of the issues involved.

It could thus be suggested that NARE has given considerable support to the redefinition of remedial education as an 'official body' within the community of remedial education. Of course, as Rudduck has commented, in respect to the influence of the National Association for the Teaching of English, it is extremely difficult to assess the degree to which such an association may influence change in teaching (1980,p.21). Not all remedial teachers, for example, are members of NARE. The survey carried out by Clunies-Ross and Wimhurst found that about a quarter of the teachers sampled were members of such professional associations, the majority being members of NARE (1983,p.98). A greater number may read the journal or be influenced by colleagues who support the views of NARE. It cannot be assumed though, that all members of NARE would necessarily agree with a new, cross-curricular approach to remedial education. Nevertheless, studies of curriculum change and of the history of subject associations would seem to suggest that such associations, or to be more precise, particular influential members of such associations, can be critical 'reality definers' for members of a subject community (Goodson,1983, Layton,1984, Cooper,1985). NARE seems to be a further example of this kind of

influence. Certainly it is possible to suggest that
without the efforts of certain members of NARE, the
changes in secondary education which were forcing
remedial education to take a new role might have
left the remedial teacher as <u>more</u> of a marginal
adjunct to secondary education, with fewer pupils to
provide remedial help for and no alternative role to
play. As it is, recognising perhaps that such
changes heralded 'the death knell of remedial
education as we have come to know it'
(McNicholas,1976,p.115), a new brief for the
remedial teacher has been articulated and developed,
positing such teachers as 'change agents', as
'partners' with subject teachers and as 'policy-
makers' across the curriculum. Thus an enhanced
status has been mooted and an extended role been
delineated which should guarantee the continued
importance of remedial work.

NARE could be considered as the main 'voice of
remedial education' which has 'led the way', through
its journal and its publications, to a new approach
to remedial work (NARE,1982). At the same time new
approaches have been supported and elaborated by
other practitioners not necessarily closely
connected with NARE and have also been given
consideration in various educational reports,
including those from HMI. The degree to which NARE
has indeed 'led the way' thus needs to be more
closely considered. The Bullock Report, for
example, suggested that the relationship between
remedial work and the general curriculum was of the
greatest importance and that closer liaison was
needed between remedial and class teacher to ensure
'follow up' of pupil progress. It also recommended
that consultation between remedial and other
teachers should be developed to ensure that work and
methods in all areas of the curriculum were suited
to pupils' particular needs and that remedial
specialists might join pupils in subject lessons to
give them support (DES,1975,Chapter 18). The
Bullock Report also mooted the development of
'Language across the Curriculum' policies. Although
English teachers rather than remedial teachers were
to play the central role in such policies, support
and encouragement was thus given to the idea of
cross-curricular work.

Further encouragement to cross-curricular
planning has since also been given by HMI in a
series of working papers entitled 'Curriculum 11-
16' (DES,1977), which proposed that school curricula
should be analysed and constructed not only in

41

regard to individual subjects. Rather, it was
suggested,

> it is necessary to look through the subject or
> discipline to areas of experience and knowledge
> to which it may provide access and to the
> skills and attitudes which it may assist to
> develop.
> (DES,ibid.,p.6)

Moreover, to facilitate the adoption of such an
approach to curriculum planning it would be
necessary

> for each faculty or subject department to
> examine what knowledge, skills, forms of
> understanding and modes of learning it can
> offer to the education of every pupil and for
> all departments together to consider how their
> various and complementary roles combine in the
> pupils' developing experience.
> (ibid.,p.7)

This approach to curriculum planning would seem to
give considerable support to the notion of a 'whole
school' or cross-curricular approach to pupil
learning and thus to the consideration of curricular
experiences of pupils with learning difficulties
both within and across subjects.

The means through which such a 'whole school'
approach to learning difficulties could be realised
have been further considered by HMI in a report on
'Slow Learning and Less Successful Pupils in
Secondary Schools' (DES,1984). This report
recommended that close links between remedial and
other staff be initiated and maintained, in order to
discuss and design work for such pupils. It also
suggested that

> it would prove beneficial to the work of the
> pupils if the organisation of a school
> facilitated these links and worked towards a
> remedial department's becoming a support
> service to a wide range of needs.
> (ibid.,p.44)

To facilitate such developments it was further
recommended that all teachers should know something
about the identification of pupils with learning
difficulties and that heads of faculties and subject
departments should receive in-service help to enable

them to contribute to the development of curricula and methodologies appropriate for children of all levels of literacy or ability. Critical comments were also made about the restricted curriculum offered to some pupils with learning difficulties and it was suggested that the training of remedial teachers should involve

> a broadening of the scope from a narrow concentration on reading difficulties to a wider range of special educational needs and approaches to meet them.
> (ibid.,p.47)

It could thus be argued that the redefinition of remedial education has received considerable support and encouragement outside of the narrower confines of NARE alone and in particular has been given the accolade of 'good practice', and thus legitimation, by HMI. At the same time, some of the most recent discussions of the curriculum which have come from HMI and the DES give less explicit support to such a redefinition. The papers on Curriculum 5-16 discuss 'areas of experience' across the curriculum but a renewed emphasis is given to discrete subject content with the publication of separate booklets on each subject. Little attention is paid to special educational needs[14]. The DES document 'The School Curriculum' (1981) discussed special schools but not 'special educational needs' in ordinary schools, thus giving little recognition to the idea of a 'continuum of provision' as mooted by the Warnock Report. Given too the interest now being devoted to new examinations, the GCSE, examinations which will not involve a large number of pupils with learning difficulties and the new emphasis on main subject training in teacher education, which may reinforce the notion that subject teachers are primarily concerned with the teaching of their subjects and not with the development of appropriate learning experiences for a variety of pupils, it could be suggested that the support and encouragement given to any redefinition of remedial education at national policy making level is somewhat questionable.

This lack of real and consistent support is even more apparent when some comparison is made with Scotland, where a more coherent and authoritative national policy seems to have emerged. In Scotland in 1978, Scottish HMI produced a report on the education of pupils with learning difficulties which was critical of traditional remedial education. It was recommended in this report that approaches to provision for pupils with learning difficulties should be restructured, within a series of wider changes in secondary education as a whole. Thus mixed ability teaching should be extended, withdrawal for remedial help be minimised, more curricular options be provided for the less able pupil and assessment be related to the capabilities of pupils. Remedial education should be more widely defined to include all children who experience a difficulty with their learning and should become a responsibility of the whole school. Remedial teachers should become consultants on appropriate materials and teaching strategies and should be involved in team teaching and advisory work across the curriculum (SED,1978). Following this report, region-wide policies were implemented which included the abolition of remedial classes and the development of teams of remedial specialists to carry out a consultative and team teaching brief (Booth,1983a).

Thus, as Jones has commented, looking at the development of remedial education in Scotland, given that Scottish HMI have called for a redefinition of remedial education, that there has been major discussion on curriculum change in Scotland and that most Scottish regions have also produced working party reports on the development of remedial education in their area, remedial education in Scotland, 'contemplating where to go in the future, has not stood alone at the crossroads'. Rather, 'it is surrounded by so many travellers whose paths have converged and whose advice, encouragement, caution, whatever, is being proferred' (1979,p.61). In contrast, remedial education south of the border could be described as more of a 'lone traveller' with occasional companions whose company and route directions are somewhat erratic and unreliable. Thus perhaps NARE has indeed 'led the way' in the development and dissemination of a redefinition of remedial education. In the absence of empirical research on the history of this redefinition, it is difficult to precisely delineate the influence of NARE and it would certainly be useful, for example, to establish the degree to which redefinition has been encouraged and moulded by pressure from remedial teachers within schools (and which schools), as well as from certain members of NARE. Equally it would be useful to examine in further detail how national and local policies have encouraged or inhibited the acceptance and implementation of a redefinition in schools. However it can perhaps be argued with some credence that NARE has been a major source of the redefinition of remedial education, aided by some 'official' support and encouragement, but not by clear and authoritative national and regional policy developments in England or Wales.

The redefinition of remedial education, therefore, cannot be explained in terms of central policy intervention[15]. The role of NARE has to be carefully considered. It is also important to examine why a particular redefinition has been mooted. The changes in secondary education which forced remedial education to take a new role may have provided a particular impetus towards reform. However they did not provide an obvious focus or direction for new developments. Indeed, if anything, they threatened the demise of remedial education. To understand, therefore, the particular substance of redefinition as it emerged, we need also to look at other features of the context of change, features which were briefly discussed in the first chapter, namely the low and marginal status of remedial education, its diversity and the limitations of traditional remedial practice.

The low and marginal status of remedial education has long since concerned many remedial teachers and does seem to have provided a particular focus, and rationales, for change. Coupled with this concern about status there has been increasing criticism of traditional practice. It has been seen as ineffective and limited. Specialised and separate tuition in the basic skills was not followed up in the mainstream classroom. The 'ambulance service' approach did not allow for changes to be made in those curricular and organisational features of schools which might be causing and certainly were exacerbating the learning difficulties of pupils. The separate teaching of basic skills was also becoming increasingly incompatible with new knowledge which suggested that such skills were best learned in context. Moreover, segregation of pupils with learning difficulties could be seen to be incompatible with comprehensive education and egalitarian principles. The redefinition of remedial education, as currently mooted, offers 'solutions' to the problems of status, of segregation and of the 'ambulance service'. Working across the curriculum allows for 'follow up' of remedial help, facilitates the

learning of basic skills in the context of subject
learning and provides opportunities for integration,
with improved content and teaching methods for
pupils with learning difficulties. The 'new
partnership' between remedial and subject teacher
also offers opportunities to offset the low and
marginal status of remedial education by meshing
such provision with the high-status academic core of
the curriculum and with the mainstream organisation
and structure of the school.

The redefinition of remedial education posits a
number of benefits to pupils through this
integration of provision. It also of course, offers
a number of benefits to remedial teachers. For
example, it provides opportunities to change
previous low and marginal status, by becoming
involved with subject teaching. In addition though,
a new and extended role has also been suggested,
whereby the remedial teacher may be considered a
'change agent', with a brief to modify and improve
the curriculum and develop 'whole school policies'.
The remedial teacher is thus cast in an implicit
(and indeed often explicit) management role. Status
(or at least, potential status) has thus been
transformed from not just marginality to 'equality'
with other subject departments but from marginality
to a role which legitimates involvement with and
possibly even some 'control' over the work of other
subject departments. Remedial teachers have, in the
past, rarely been successful in the annual auctions
of staffing, resources and policy attention within
schools. The bid for status and importance, now
finally made, is for an exceptionally high stake[16].

Whether such a bid will be successful is
another question. It is also a matter of equal
debate as to whether the current diversity of
remedial education will be overcome. Such diversity
has in the past been perceived as an additional
weakness, a possibly contributory factor to low and
marginal status and ineffective practice. The
consistency and unity of purpose offered by this new
definition of 'good practice' could therefore be
viewed as providing an additional impetus towards
change. The possibility of realising such goals and
overcoming the legacies of diversity, marginality
and ineffective practice will now be discussed.

THE IMPLEMENTATION OF REDEFINED REMEDIAL EDUCATION

One of the significant elements of the context of

46

redefinition therefore, concerns the diversity of policies and practices subsumed under the aegis of remedial education. In tracing the emergence of a redefinition, it would thus be important to discover whether pressures for change have come from remedial teachers in particular types of school with particular curricular and organisational contexts and whether experiences of particular policies for remedial provision have engendered more dissatisfaction with the status quo than others. Such research would then provide some empirical grounding for the proposition that certain changes in secondary education, coupled with certain dissatisfactions about traditional policies, status and practice, have indeed provided the impetus for redefinition, despite the apparent diversity of provision. In addition though, this diversity poses another question, namely that of the consequences of redefinition. It may well be the case that the diversity which has been characteristic of traditional approaches will equally be a feature of redefinition.

It is of course a now widely recognised feature of educational innovation that the implementation of new curricula or pedagogies will not necessarily lead to similar results in each implementing school. Studies of the implementation of curriculum projects such as those developed by the Schools Council and Nuffield have shown how elements of these projects are often modified by innovating schools, in terms of both content and pedagogy and thus it cannot be assumed that change will take place in accordance with every intention of the innovators. Some diversity in the case of remedial education could thus be expected. Such experiences have also led to the questioning of methods of innovation which depend on the conveyance of a ready-made project to user schools and to a greater consideration of the context of innovation, in particular the views and prior practices of teachers who will be involved[17].

The lessons of past innovation, in particular the need to acknowledge the innovating context as a significant feature of change, have important implications for the redefinition of remedial education and will shortly be further discussed. It is also important though to consider whether the redefinition of remedial education represents a particularly problematic case of change, not just because of the traditional diversity of policies and practice found in remedial education, nor because of the general diversity of schools, but because of the particular nature of the redefinition itself. To take one example, for instance, of the particular type of redefinition being mooted here, the redefinition of remedial education is not a redefinition of subject content which can be tangibly perceived in terms of new textbooks or new examination syllabi. It differs therefore from redefinitions which have taken place in science or mathematics where the textbook has been a major initiating device of change (Cooper,1982,1985) and for that matter, from redefinitions in other subject areas where textbooks (or packs of teaching materials) and new examination syllabi are often available to indicate and codify precisely what new content is being mooted, and often, how it should be taught. Such materials, and related examination syllabi, provide at least some initial unity to redefinition, even if during the course of implementation in individual schools, or LEAs, some diversity and some modifications emerge.

The redefinition of remedial education, as currently elaborated at least, although generally concerned with the content of learning and changes in pedagogy which would render subjects more accessible to pupils with learning difficulties, offers no precise prescriptions as to the nature of that content or pedagogy. General advice as to appropriate approaches may be suggested, for example, that the readability of texts should be considered, that concrete examples should be deployed to teach ideas and concepts, that certain resources and courses may be particularly useful. Equally it may be suggested that work for pupils with learning difficulties should be individualised, should be put on tapes or special worksheets to overcome literacy problems, that a remedial teacher should give support in the mainstream class, in conjunction with the subject teacher or that certain elements of the curriculum should be modified for certain pupils[18]. However specific course content or modes of instruction are not delineated as a necessary element of redefinition. Rather such specifications are left as the outcome of collaborative work between remedial and subject teacher and collaborative curriculum planning at 'whole school' level. Given the variations in approaches to remedial work amongst remedial teachers and the concomitant variations in the teaching of subjects (both content and pedagogy) amongst subject teachers, a whole range of curricular materials, teaching methods and curricular patterns could well emerge.

A similar point could be made about the role of remedial teachers. It has already been suggested that the role of remedial teachers has not been closely defined, particularly in respect to the allocation of staff and time to the various responsibilities now deemed to belong to remedial teachers. As the redefinition of remedial education is implemented, the structure of responsibilities may thus vary between schools, even though there may be some common acceptance of the tenets of the new approach. Equally, given that the definition of the remedial teacher's pupil clientele is very broad and flexible, there may be considerable variation in respect to the identification of pupils considered to have learning difficulties (or 'special educational needs') and the number of such pupils for whom some form of special provision is made. The extent and organisation of remedial education may thus differ widely. Similarly, 'whole school policies' may vary from fairly closely prescribed approaches across the curriculum to general statements of aims giving considerable latitude in practice, at classroom level, to remedial and subject teachers.

To some extent, the issues surrounding the specific and detailed implementation of redefined remedial education do have to be related to individual schools, as much will depend on the 'needs' of pupils in a particular school and on the degree and direction of required curricular and organisational change. Given the now recognised weaknesses of a 'top-down' or 'ready-made product to user school' model of innovation, it would not be appropriate to make absolute prescriptions as to how redefinition should be implemented or indeed what are its most important components in a particular school. Nevertheless, the redefinition of remedial education, as currently constituted, does pose particular problems in respect to codifying what is entailed, since only consequent to implementation perhaps, in a variety of school contexts, will it be possible to give a more detailed flesh to the present skeletal outline of suggested 'good practice'. There are few empirical yardsticks or frameworks, in the form of textbooks, workschemes or syllabi which could be used to more closely elaborate, examine and define the crucial elements of redefinition and mark the extent of individual modifications at school and LEA level.

Moreover, unlike most subject redefinitions,

the redefinition of remedial education is highly
dependent on change in many areas of the curriculum
and requires acceptance and implementation by
members of a number of subject communities. It is
thus likely to be prone to the influence of a number
of teachers' beliefs and practices, not just those
of a particular grouping within the school. It
would also seem to require change at the
institutional level, in terms of the development of
'whole school policies', with their concomitant
implications for curriculum planning, and changes in
teaching methods, in relationships between staff and
in resource allocation. It may thus be far more
open to the influence of particular school contexts
and definitions of 'good practice'. Finally, the
redefinition of remedial education is concerned with
the securement of new outcomes. In themselves, the
redefinition of the remedial teacher's role, of
clientele, of the content and context of remedial
work and of the remedial teacher's expertise are in
a sense only a means to another end, namely changes
in provision for pupils with learning difficulties
across the curriculum. Therefore, perhaps more than
in most cases of curriculum change and subject
redefinition, the substance and processes of
redefinition itself and of its realisation or
implementation are inextricably linked.

Thus a number of issues need to be put on the
agenda of enquiry and of practice. Firstly given
the diversity of policies, practice and school
contexts endemic to traditional provision and also
potentially enshrined in redefinition, it has to be
considered whether the redefinition of remedial
education is indeed a pertinent, let alone a
unifying, issue within the community of remedial
education as a whole. This will involve examination
of the degree to which redefinition has been
accepted by community members, and for what reasons,
and how, and in which schools. This chapter has
focused on the influence of NARE as a critical
'reality definer' for remedial teachers, as the
'voice of remedial education' in its position as an
'official body'. It is not clear, however, how
representative NARE is of all remedial teachers and
teacher trainers, nor indeed whether those who have
actually been leading members of NARE and have
particularly contributed to redefinition are
themselves representative to all NARE members. Thus
to make a more detailed and considered examination
of the process and history of this redefinition,
including an examination of the role of NARE and its

influence on community members, it will be important to discover more about the views of remedial teachers and in order to further assess the sources of change, find out far more about individual school and LEA policies, what new approaches have been mooted and when they were suggested and whether local (and national) policy directions have thus also been influential. Then it may be easier to assess whether NARE has indeed been a 'segment with a mission'[19] within the community of remedial education or whether it has articulated a groundswell of demands for change and has also responded to local and national policy initiatives.

Such questions are not only of academic or historical importance. For despite apparent interest in new approaches to remedial education, at least from members of NARE (Gains and McNicholas,1981) few schools seem to have implemented a cross-curricular, collaborative pattern of remedial work. Surveys by HMI of secondary and remedial provision found few examples of an advisory or team teaching role being exercised by remedial teachers (DES,1979,1984). Similar findings were reported in a study carried out for the National Foundation for Education Research, where it was suggested that in only 21 out of 791 schools surveyed was this sort of approach being implemented (Clunies-Ross and Wimhurst,1983,p.70). It would seem to be very important to establish whether this apparent paucity of new approaches is a consequence of remedial teachers' unwillingness to redefine remedial education or is due to constraints and limitations which have impinged on desires for change. Bailey (1981) in his survey of remedial teachers found that some were indeed reluctant to take on a wider remit and work with subject teachers in the classroom. It certainly cannot be assumed that the redefinition of remedial education has gained, or reflects, wide acceptance of new concepts of the remedial teacher's role.

The question of implementation raises further problematic issues, requiring more research and discussion. Firstly, if study of the implementation of redefined remedial education is necessary to the full understanding of the substance of redefinition, then there will have to be far more research in a variety of implementing schools accompanied perhaps by the collation and dissemination of many more accounts of individual school policies and practice. In addition, if the innovating context is a significant factor in implementing redefined remedial education, then it would seem important to examine how particular school contexts do affect implementation and investigate what features of schools may facilitate or impede particular aspects of redefinition, or indeed the whole development of change in remedial provision. Above all perhaps, there is a need for further discussion and research on the views of participants, namely the remedial teachers, the pupils, management staff and in particular, the subject teacher who will be directly involved in the 'new partnership'. For although implementation of redefined remedial education does seem to be a school-based form of curriculum development, with collaboration and discussion as major strategies for change, thus avoiding some of the pitfalls which 'top-down' and 'ready-made' projects have encountered in the past, there is a sense in which it is an innovation which has been already prepared and now has to be disseminated and 'sold' to user/receivers. This redefinition has been primarily developed and articulated by remedial teachers: it has not originated from joint discussion and collaboration within individual schools, between the remedial and subject teachers who will be concerned. As such, the issue of whether it will be welcomed by other participants, whether it is congruent with their perceptions, views and practices, remains very much to the fore and it may well be the case, as with many other innovations, that responses will be shaped and even constrained by those perceptions, views and practices. Thus the perspectives of potential participants, particularly the potential 'partners', the subject teachers, would seem to be a crucial area for research.

The question of participants other than the remedial teacher, together with the question of the innovating context, the school and its wider setting, highlight another crucial aspect of the implementation of redefined remedial education, namely the means through which it will be realised, especially the influences and resources which can be brought to bear. It has already been suggested that the loci for change, namely the role of the remedial teacher, the 'partnership' between remedial and subject teacher and the development of 'whole school policies' could benefit from a more detailed and critical scrutiny. Whatever the emphasis given to 'partnerships' and 'whole school policies' and thus joint, collaborative development of remedial education across the curriculum, it would seem that the remedial teacher, as 'consultant', 'coordinator', 'change agent' or 'partner' is likely to be of crucial importance in the innovation. However the degree to which remedial teachers will be successful in the dissemination of their expertise and in the development of policy will not only be dependent on new knowledge and new skills, even though these may be important. Resources, status and power may be equally crucial. However remedial education has traditionally only enjoyed a low and marginal status, often accompanied by inadequate resources. It may well be the case that the legacies of such low status and resources, and their concomitant lack of power, may impinge on the possibilities of influence and change, particularly since the educational context of low status and resources, namely the domination of subject hierarchies and the emphasis given to academic achievement and examinations, still continues to be maintained in schools.

In addition, the questions of power and influence are important in respect to other aspects of the implementation of redefined remedial education. The support of headteachers and other management staff may be needed to facilitate the development of 'whole school policies' and ensure the concomitant provision of staffing and resources. Staff appointments, of both remedial and other teachers willing to implement the new approach to remedial provision, may similarly be dependent on headteachers and other management staff. NARE may have the resources to disseminate a redefinition of remedial education through its organisation, journal and conferences but it cannot legislate for the appointment of teachers who accept the importance of the new approach. Thus redefinition, in practice, may depend on wide acceptance of the tenets of the new approach, both within individual schools, and at LEA and national policy level as well, for otherwise the constraints of staffing, resources and definitions of 'good practice' may well militate against, as well as facilitate the implementation of redefinition. Certainly a positive outcome cannot be assumed to be inevitable, particularly in a climate of financial stringencies, with no authoritative policy directions at national level and in a context of secondary schooling which is somewhat inhibitive of change in this particular area of provision.

Thus many issues surrounding the redefinition and implementation of new approaches to remedial education remain unresolved. However a greater clarity of thinking in respect to some of the implications of redefinition, together with considerably more research and discussion, may facilitate some successful programmes for change. The rest of this book will therefore be concerned with some of the issues of redefinition and its implementation which have been raised in this chapter, drawing on both my own[20] and other research. Given the diversity of schools, policies and practice as a context for change, it should perhaps be noted that my research data, as reported in the following chapters, is not being presented as necessarily typical of all schools, or typical of all views of subject and remedial teachers or typical of all interactions which might take place in collaborative work. Nor does it represent an attempt to present a series of case studies of particular schools. Rather, the data is presented as illustration to a number of suggested possible dimensions and features of redefinition which could be considered by both remedial teachers working in their own schools and by researchers interested in pursuing further enquiry. It is hoped to thus stimulate further debate by bringing a number of theoretical and practical problems to notice. Above all it is hoped that thereby remedial teachers will be encouraged to look beyond their own specific experiences and perspectives to take some cognisance of both the perspectives and practices of others and also of the social context in which new approaches to remedial education will be developed and implemented. Thus the next chapter will start this exploration with some consideration of the context of potential collaboration across the curriculum, namely with the questions surrounding subject teaching and pupils with learning difficulties.

NOTES

1. The name of the NARE journal has now also been changed, in conjunction with the name of NARE (see Note 1, Chapter One).

2. There are of course many other contributions to the redefinition of remedial education which have not been discussed. No denigration is intended to those contributions in the choice of examples and accounts which has been made.

3. A number of different terms are used to describe such 'partnerships' and 'whole school

policies', such as 'support' work, the 'whole school approach' etc. The terms 'partnership' and 'whole school policies' will be primarily used in this book to summarise such developments.

4. The latest guidelines from NARE could thus be seen as an attempt to further redefine remedial education in the light of the Warnock Report and the 1981 Education Act.

5. It could well be therefore that professional responsibilities for 'special educational needs' will be split between former remedial teachers now taking on a new role in 'ordinary' schools and other 'special' teachers being primarily concerned with 'special' schools or units, the very distinction it was hoped would be eradicated with the new concepts and approaches. Certainly there has not, as yet, been the amalgamation of the professional associations of 'remedial' and 'special' education teachers which might offset such distinctions.

6. See the contributions to redefinition previously discussed.

7. See Chapter One.

8. See Cave and Maddison (1978) for a more detailed discussion of these developments.

9. The influence of such research is of course difficult to estimate. However the switch in emphasis, within the sociology of education, towards the 'black box' of schooling, would seem to be important in terms of the issues and research findings it has raised. A similar point could be made about 'school effectiveness' research, such as that of Rutter, Maughan, Mortimore and Ouston (1979).

10. The degree to which such 'experiential' approaches (as represented by, for example, heuristic science teaching, practical and field work in geography or the new emphasis on the use of primary sources and issues of 'evidence' and 'bias' rather than 'fact' in history) have indeed penetrated the secondary curriculum is perhaps open to question. However at least such approaches posit the importance of 'process' in learning.

11. Such arguments have been used in relation to integrating pupils from special schools and may well have been equally important in respect to the integration of pupils already in ordinary schools but holding a marginal position or experiencing some segregation through withdrawal or special classes.

12. As Cooper argues, it is important to 'make possible the articulation of structural and

interactional levels of analysis' when looking at subject redefinition (1983,p.208). A focus on the interactional level would need to include analysis of how the redefinition of remedial education has been argued and developed within the community of remedial education, the conflicts and alliances involved and the resources available to different groups within the community. Such detail is not currently available to facilitate such an analysis. However the focus on the role of NARE and of members of the community of remedial education within this chapter may provide a useful starting point and does suggest that redefinition cannot merely be seen as a product of structural change.

13. Now called Support for Learning (see Note 1).

14. It is argued that because the goals of education apply to all pupils and all types of school, 'special needs' are not to be singled out (1985b,p.5). However this approach does lead to neglect of the many modifications in curricula which may be made for 'special needs' and which do need specific discussion.

15. Except perhaps in relation to the further redefinition of remedial education now being mooted in the light of the Warnock Report and the 1981 Education Act, which further redefinition could be seen to be, in part at least, a response to legislative and policy changes. Remedial education may therefore be a rare example of 'undirected' change given increasing central intervention in the 'secret garden' of the rest of the curriculum (Lawton,1980). However there are signs that the lack of intervention in the education of the 'less able' and pupils with learning difficulties may be changing, especially with the development of schemes such as TVEI and the 'Low Attainers Project' currently being sponsored by the DES.

16. It would seem therefore that the redefinition of remedial education, like other examples of curriculum change, can be viewed as the pursuit of material interests (cf.Goodson,1983). However the claims to 'academic' status and resources are to be realised through an association with 'academic' subjects, rather than by the emergence of a 'new' subject freed of its former low status and traditions. The limitations of only being associated with academic subjects, rather than having a discrete position within the curriculum, will be overcome with the legitimation given to the involvement of the remedial teacher in cross-

curricular work.

17. See MacDonald and Walker (1976) for a more detailed discussion of these issues and experiences.

18. Chapter Three looks at some of these suggestions in relation to the teaching of subjects. They may also be found in the literature on learning difficulties, in accounts of redefinition and in publications from NARE (e.g. NARE,1983).

19. It has been suggested (e.g. Ball,1983, Cooper,1983,1985) that subject communities can be viewed as analogous to professions, particularly as conceptualised by Bucher and Strauss, namely as 'loose amalgamations of segments pursuing different objectives in different manners and more or less delicately held together under a common name at a particular period in history' (1976,p.19). Different segments may well have different 'missions'. Given the diversity of remedial education, this model would seem to be pertinent to the community of remedial education: the issue is then to what degree NARE is but a segment of the whole community (or indeed segmented itself) and how much the 'mission' of redefining remedial education reflects the aspirations, beliefs and interests of all community members.

20. This research is now being prepared for a D.Phil thesis entitled 'The Redefinition of Remedial Education' to be submitted in late 1986 at the Department of Educational Studies, University of Oxford. The research project consisted of interviews with subject and remedial teachers working in six comprehensive schools in one LEA, together with some observation, and further interviews with heads, deputy heads and LEA staff. The limitations of the 'decontextualised' approach to data reporting and analysis used in this book are acknowledged but it was considered that given the book's main purpose, namely to encourage debate, rather than report on case studies, such an approach might be more appropriate. The research focused on the subjects of English, mathematics, history, geography, science and modern languages since it is in these areas that pupils' learning difficulties have been regarded to be most acute and where most attention and collaborative work between remedial and subject teacher has been concentrated. The importance of other areas of the curriculum is acknowledged and further research 'across the curriculum' is urgently required.

Chapter Three

SUBJECT TEACHING AND PUPILS WITH LEARNING
DIFFICULTIES

The redefinition of remedial education posits a 'new
partnership' between remedial and subject teacher to
facilitate the sharing of expertise and the
development of appropriate materials and methods for
the teaching of subjects to pupils with learning
difficulties. Such pupils may well receive more
help and support from remedial teachers in the
mainstream classroom, through the use of team
teaching arrangements rather than withdrawal tuition
or special classes. To implement such collaborative
work, remedial teachers will need a greater
understanding of the ways in which subject teachers
view and assess pupils with learning difficulties
and of the problems which such pupils may experience
in different subjects. They will also need some
knowledge of the strategies and methods employed by
subject teachers to teach such pupils, for such
strategies and methods, together with subject
teachers' perceptions or constructs of learning
difficulties, are likely to influence both the mode
and the outcome of collaborative work.

However the need for such knowledge raises a
number of problems. Very little research has been
carried out on these aspects of subject teaching.
Many remedial teachers may also have limited recent
experience of subject teaching. It may thus be
difficult to construct these new 'partnerships' and
ways of working which are congruent with the
perceptions, strategies and methods of both subject
and remedial teachers and which ensure that
provision for pupils is effective. If more
information and research were available, the process
of developing such 'partnerships' could be aided.
Certainly it would seem important that remedial
teachers concerned to work across the curriculum
should become more conversant with relevant aspects

of such teaching, in order to choose the most effective strategies for change.

This chapter will therefore focus on some aspects of subject teaching and pupils with learning difficulties. In the absence of detailed research it is difficult to draw a definitive picture of the range of learning difficulties and of subject teacher's constructs of such pupils, the process of assessment and typification and the variety of approaches and strategies which may be employed in the classroom. Nevertheless a number of subject specialists have written about the teaching of pupils with learning difficulties and there have been a few surveys of policies and practice. During my own research I also asked subject teachers about their perceptions of learning difficulties, the problems experienced in teaching such pupils and methods and strategies employed. The available literature and some of my own research data will therefore be used as a starting point for discussion.

SUBJECT TEACHERS' CONSTRUCTS OF PUPILS WITH LEARNING DIFFICULTIES

The way in which subject teachers view pupils with learning difficulties, or in other words, their constructs of such pupils, would seem to be a particularly important aspect of any collaborative work between remedial and subject teacher for such constructs may influence identification and assessment, referrals and requests for remedial help and choice of teaching methods and strategies. From analysis of the available literature and my own research data it could be suggested that there appear to be a number of dimensions to such constructs, reflecting concern with pupils' attainments in basic skills, their capacities to grasp concepts, knowledge and skills, and also their learning characteristics, attitudes, motivation and behaviour. Meshed in with such general concerns can also be found subject-specific dimensions, relating to the particular requirements of individual subjects.

Thus the English teachers whom I interviewed were concerned with basic literacy skills, with learning characteristics such as ability to concentrate and motivation, and also with creativity and imagination, which could be seen to be particularly crucial to participation in English lessons and to the production of 'good' English work. As one English teacher commented:

> Forgetting the mechanics, on the creative side the problem is the development of an idea. Some of them (pupils with learning difficulties) have very good outlines but they end up as outlines, not for example putting feelings and thoughts in.

This concern with creativity and self-expression was similarly raised by another English teacher who suggested that pupils with learning difficulties lacked the capacity to write effective descriptions:

> I mean you could describe Blackpool seafront itself beautifully but they see it in terms of candyfloss and rides, they are not introspective, they are rather passive, are not fired up, they don't say 'It's the greatest experience'.

Technical difficulties such as poor reading skills could impede enjoyment or understanding of a novel read in class whilst poor spelling and punctuation were not only viewed as an intrinsic problem but seen to impinge on capacity for self-expression and communication of ideas to others. Thus although it is possible to discern a trend in English teaching which stresses that cognitive difficulties are not necessarily reflected in weak sensibilities (e.g. Stratta,1964, Holbrook,1968) and English is often viewed not so much as a subject or series of skills to be learned so much as a process of personal development and growth (Shayer,1972, Mathieson,1975), some pupils may still be seen to have difficulties because of the restricted capacities and skills which they bring to lessons. The low literacy skills, limited vocabulary, poor imagination and difficulties with understanding words, language structures and concepts which have been identified as being significant to English teaching and learning (e.g. Creber,1984) may thus be important dimensions of English teachers' constructs of pupils with learning difficulties.

Mathematics teachers on the other hand seem to be concerned with different skills and concepts. The teachers I interviewed mentioned problems with place value, with the four rules of number, with mathematical vocabulary and with the abstract and difficult nature of some mathematical concepts.

Such problems were seen to be further compounded by lack of attention and concentration, poor retention and in many instances, low motivation. Previous mathematical learning and experience was also seen to be problematic: basic rules had not been mastered or had been learned by rote with little understanding. Remediation then became difficult because of pupil expectations and embarrassment. However because of the structure of mathematics, where new learning depended on the grasp of progressive concepts, such basic knowledge had to be mastered. Two different mathematics teachers elaborated these problems thus:

> A lot of difficulties come from being taught to do an arithmetical task by rote with no understanding of why they are actually doing it. So they tend to fail. You then have to go back to basics, to number bonds and so on, what we tend to think of as primary school work. As we go up we tend to expect children of a certain age to do certain things and they can't. And then there is also an embarrassment factor - who wants to be counting bricks when they are eleven?

> It's often difficult when you have got pupils who have got lost with some of the basic concepts early on. If you go back to the early concepts, they have done this before and already are not interested, think they are going to fail again. But because of the hierarchy of the subject, most of the new things rely on those basics.

This concern with lack of basic concepts and skills possessed by pupils with learning difficulties and the implications which it has for further mathematical learning is also reflected in the literature written by subject specialists. In addition, writers such as Stockwell (1975) comment on the limited memory and attention span of pupils with learning difficulties, their social immaturity, irregular attendance and a tendency to be easily distracted. Choat (1974) mentions limited visual perceptions and a restricted mathematical vocabulary. Larcombe (1985) is particularly concerned with the syndrome of reinforced failure, leading to low self-esteem and with the legacies of inappropriate teaching. He also mentions difficulties arising from possession of only a limited repertoire of mathematical information and skills, problems with making connections and transfers to new situations, lack of confidence, difficulties with abstract thought and patterns of work avoidance. Bailey (1979) discusses difficulties with vocabulary and concepts, confusion over arithmetical signs, poor auditory memory, problems with visual sequencing, difficulties with abstract thinking and inability to transfer mechanical computation skills to problems whilst Berrill (1982) considers that weaknesses in intellectual skills, adverse attitudes and a poor self-image may all contribute to learning difficulties. The Schools Council Low Attainers in Mathematics Project (Denvir, Stolz and Brown,1982) reports a variety of mathematical problems and suggests that the only common characteristic of such pupils may be low attainment in mathematics. Teachers and advisers questioned cited a number of reasons for such difficulties, including physical or sensory defects, emotional and behavioural problems, anxiety, slowness in grasping ideas, poor reading ability, difficulty with oral expression or written work, absence from school, an impoverished home background and inappropriate teaching. The Cockcroft Report (DES,1982), it should perhaps be noted, suggested that reasons for low attainment could include lack of confidence, inappropriate teaching and poor reading skills. Low attainment was also seen to be associated with low general ability (Paras.334-5).

In respect to history, Cowie (1980) has identified a number of problems experienced by what she terms 'slow learning children'. She notes that most pupils may have language difficulties in history, due to its reliance on the full range of past tenses and on the conditional clause and subjunctive mode for hypothetical and exploratory thinking. Historical texts also employ complex sentences, often with qualifying subordinate clauses. However the slow learning child may need particular help with this sort of language. It is also suggested that a lack of background and general knowledge and depth of personal experience may inhibit learning in history as may weaknesses in long-term memory and difficulties with abstract concepts. McIver (1982) mentions the problems of poor attainments in reading and writing, poor retention, short attention span, lack of motivation, limited powers of discussion and difficulties with skill and concept development. Hallam (1982) considers that teachers should be aware of pupils' differing stages of intellectual development and suggests that pupils with learning difficulties may on average be two years behind their peers in terms of the stage of thinking they have achieved. Thus they may not cope easily with the more abstract concepts of history such as time. Wilson (1982b) considers that a failure to master language and communicate effectively is one of the most serious general problems of the 'slow learner' but has particular implications for history, which depends so much on reading and writing and has high linguistic demands. The history teachers whom I interviewed were similarly particularly concerned with reading and writing difficulties, with problems of specialised vocabulary and historical text and with the limitations of general knowledge and experience held by pupils with learning difficulties. They also mentioned difficulties with the retention of information, with eliciting information from texts, with self expression and with understanding how the world really was in the past.

Geography teachers were also concerned with literacy and language difficulties, including those arising from the specialised vocabulary and concepts of the subject. Pupils with learning difficulties were also seen to have problems with generalisation and the handling of information and concepts, as one teacher explained:

> Pupils really need to absorb information, remember it, then apply it in another situation, which they find very difficult. The best can, the average have difficulty remembering what the facts were in the first place, let alone applying it to another situation and this is where the kids with problems really fall down.

Difficulties with mapping skills such as scale representation and recognising the shape of countries were also mentioned. A survey carried out by Corney and Rawling (1982) on the views of geography teachers in relation to teaching less able 11-14 year olds suggests that geography teachers are particularly concerned with reading, writing and numeracy difficulties and with problems of concentration and retention. About half the teachers questioned also felt that lack of motivation, behaviour problems and poor attendance were related to learning difficulties. In respect to the characteristics of geography providing problems for pupils, many teachers in this survey referred at length to difficulties with using maps and the understanding of geographical facts and ideas was also seen as problematic. Pupils were seen to have difficulties with the understanding of distant places, with generalising from case studies and with recognising patterns or drawing out relationships and ideas. Some teachers also considered that field work posed problems for pupils with learning difficulties although others considered that observation and data collection could be carried out successfully. Boardman, in his introductory contribution to a number of articles written by geographers on 'Geography with Slow Learners' (Boardman, 1982) suggests that the main problem of such pupils is a limited ability to deal with new situations by making use of earlier experiences and previously acquired concepts. Moreover since such pupils function at a lower intellectual level than other pupils, they also take longer to master skills and comprehend ideas and have greater difficulty with abstract concepts. The retention of factual information is also seen to be a problem by Boardman, as are limited attention and concentration spans and a disorganised approach to work. Booth (1980) calls attention to the difficulties caused by a low level of basic skills and by discipline and behaviour problems, problems which are seen to arise from lack of confidence or from an inability or unwillingness to see the relevance of work being done. Booth also suggests that pupils with learning difficulties have problems with abstract ideas and with things which are outside their direct personal experience. Thus given that maps and models are abstractions and geographical examples often come from outside pupils' direct experience, the teaching of such pupils can raise particular problems for geographers.

In an article on the teaching of science with 'pupils of low educational achievement', Clegg and Morley (1980) suggest that such pupils have low powers of thought and retention and tend to be poorly motivated. Kershaw and Scott (1975) make similar comments about such pupils. Hinson (1982) raises the question of specialist vocabulary and suggests that pupils with learning difficulties need time to acquire the meaning of such specialist words. He also argues that such pupils are limited

to the use of concrete operational thinking and thus
will have difficulty with some of the requirements
of secondary science - for example the need to
confirm a hypothesis from experimental evidence. It
is perhaps worth noting in this context that
although the work of Shayer and Adey (1981) is not
specifically concerned with pupils with learning
difficulties, they do suggest that there is a
considerable mismatch between the cognitive demands
of secondary science curricula and pupils'
development, a problem which has been exacerbated by
the adoption of heuristic approaches to science
teaching. Dallas (1980) makes a similar point about
the teaching of biology to 'less able pupils' and
also comments that lack of retention may be a
particular problem. The science teachers whom I
interviewed seemed to be similarly concerned with
problems of retention, of specialist vocabulary and
difficulties with abstract concepts and
generalisation. Competence in handling experiments
and equipment was also sometimes seen to be limited,
with pupils having difficulties in following
instructions or recording what they had done.

The modern languages teachers I spoke to were
also concerned about the problem of retention and in
addition with poor concentration, particularly where
listening to oral work was concerned. As one
teacher explained:

> They need listening skills and where these are
> poor it is a problem. They have to listen all
> the time, not like other lessons where they can
> lose concentration but then return to work or
> where because it is the English language, they
> can listen to one word and guess two.

It was also suggested that because modern languages
were often difficult for such pupils, they
frequently lost motivation. The modern languages
teachers were also very concerned about language
skills in general and with the difficulties created
by pupils not knowing ideas and concepts in English,
so that these could not be tackled in a foreign
language either. Smith (1973) has also suggested
that 'less able' pupils have difficulties due to
short concentration span, lack of motivation to
learn a language, poor short-term and long-term
memory, poor auditory discrimination and problems
with the making of linguistic analogies. Lewis
(1973) argues that the nature of language learning
presents problems, in that languages are linear and

cumulative and instruction is highly intensive but nevertheless 'slow learners' do not necessarily have particular problems with retention, listening, attention span or reading difficulties. Murray (1980) mentions the problem of motivation and Hawkins (1979) identifies particular difficulties with the recognition of language patterns and with retention.

This brief review would seem to suggest that subject teachers' constructs of pupils with learning difficulties are somewhat diverse in that they are related to the various skills and knowledge of different subjects. However they also have some common features. There is a common concern with basic skills, with intellectual abilities and with learning characteristics such as concentration or retention. The concern with basic skills could be seen to reflect their importance in the learning of all subjects and a similar point could be made about intellectual abilities and learning characteristics. Such constructs are also comparative in nature, related to the 'normal performance' which could be expected of pupils at different ages in different subjects. Unfortunately such comparison then implies a 'deficit' in pupils with learning difficulties, that they are less able or competent than their peers. Moreover such 'deficits' are seen to be an individual problem, not necessarily related to the way in which certain subjects are defined or taught[1]. Pupils with learning difficulties are also seen to be unable to 'engage' with 'what really counts' as the subject, whether this involves being a creative writer in English lessons, or a 'good scientist', able to deduce conclusions from experimental work and grasp abstract concepts. However it is the teacher's definition of the subject which is posed as meaningful and important. The pupil's view or definition of what may count as 'good work' is not given consideration[2].

It is also important to note that such constructs may not necessarily reflect pupils' actual difficulties in lessons. Such constructs may be based on stereotypical or unexplored assumptions about the problems presented by pupils with learning difficulties. In addition a concern with particular aspects of subject learning may be obscuring other and equally pertinent problems. Of course much of what has been written or said about pupils' difficulties does represent considerable teaching experience and in questioning the veracity of such constructs, it is not being suggested that they are neither useful nor appropriate. More knowledge of subject teachers' views could well help to identify pupils' problems and ways of overcoming them in lessons. Nevertheless, much more research would seem to be needed before definitive conclusions are drawn about pupils' learning difficulties in subject lessons[3].

What does seem to be clear is that such learning difficulties cannot be construed as problems which are located in individuals and their 'deficits' alone. Such difficulties are grounded in certain social definitions of knowledge and certain social assumptions about relevant characteristics and behaviours. They also take their form and substance from certain social situations of teaching and learning. Such learning difficulties can therefore be seen to be 'socially constructed'. Further research on pupils' difficulties will therefore have to consider not only the individual characteristics, skills and knowledge of pupils but the way in which these are rendered problematic in particular subjects and lessons, in particular teaching and learning situations. Some further aspects of such teaching and learning, and their relationship to learning difficulties, will now be discussed.

THE MANGEMENT OF TEACHING AND LEARNING

It has been suggested that subject teachers' constructs of pupils with learning difficulties are in part related to the perceived demands, skills, content and pedagogy of different subjects and are thus embedded within the context of the classroom. Such a relationship to subject and classroom context and to pedagogical concerns can also be found in subject teachers' perceptions of the 'management problems' presented by pupils with learning difficulties. The teachers whom I interviewed made a number of comments about management problems, including those of dealing with a range of ability and pacing and of having enough time and expertise to help such pupils. A science teacher, for example, described some of his problems as follows:

> They (pupils with learning difficulties) don't have enough time and I don't devote enough time to them. When I have got a full class, say a third year class, and there are three of them (pupils with learning difficulties) in there, I

explain something, everything is being set up, they come to me and they say 'What shall we do?' I say, 'You will have to wait' because for safety's sake I have got to watch the majority, because there are always one or two who might like to short things out or whatever. They could then justifiably turn around and say 'You are not helping us'. I know I don't and I feel guilty about it. Once everyone has sat down and all the practical is out, I can go to them. But by then they are sticking out, because everyone is doing it and they are not. So I have to go over and everyone can see I am having to go so they feel even more embarrassed, that 'We are remedial and don't understand'. Then I explain and they go and get their apparatus, they may find it is all gone or in bits elsewhere so that get's sorted out and I am half helping them and half the middle of the road (pupils) and they are saying 'Sir, my apparatus doesn't work, I'm stuck'. I know they need someone sitting with them, or with a little group, 'Look those who have problems, come over here'.

Such experience was not unique to science lessons, where practical work might be seen to take up a lot of teacher time. A geography teacher, for example, also described the difficulties of giving enough attention to all pupils:

In one of my second year classes, the range of ability is quite tremendous, I have four girls who will do everything and anything and it is always done perfectly and they have often finished their work before the lads at the other end have found their pens and pencils or been given their pens and pencils and put pen to paper to start. This is the eternal problem, finding work that will keep all the kids productively occupied all the time, because the better kids suffer in a way from lack of attention. You know that if you set some work, they will get on and do it and you will have to spend most of your time, depending on the number of remedial kids, most of your time with them, showing them what to do and how to do it, holding their hands and so on. The other kids don't get the attention they deserve in a way.

Similar points were made by teachers of other subjects, most of whom had considerable teaching experience. Such difficulties cannot thus just be imputed to particular subject pedagogies or limited teaching experience. Why then do such difficulties occur?

Teaching involves a number of tasks. It can be conceptualised as a process of mediation between an array of 'goods' such as knowledge and skills and the capabilities which pupils or students have for understanding and coming to terms with such goods (Westbury,1973,p.101). However whereas in the individual tutorial, the tutor can search for the place the student is at and then take him or her through a series of experiences designed to lead to learning, the classroom

> has a number of students who are at different states of readiness for the particular learning at hand, have different ability levels, different enthusiasms, and, inevitably, differing willingnesses to attend, here and now, to this particular topic.
> (Westbury,ibid.)

Thus the tasks of 'pitching' material and explanations and planning pupil progress are made more complex by pupil differences in the large classroom group and greater pupil numbers will invariably bring up problems of the allocation of the teacher's time and attention. Pupils with learning difficulties are seen to exacerbate the difficulty of such tasks because they frequently do not understand the work that the majority can grasp. They then need extra attention for explanation or different materials, demands which impinge on the scarce resource of the teacher's time. Or such pupils may not have the requisite skills (for example, to set up science equipment correctly, as described by the science teacher just quoted) and so need extra help to ensure they can begin or continue the lesson. As the geography teacher just quoted suggested, they may also work more slowly than most pupils, thus upsetting the schedule and planning of a lesson, both in respect to completing their individual work and in terms of generating problems of 'keeping everybody occupied'. They may also need extra teacher attention because of poor concentration or low motivation.

Pupils with learning difficulties are thus seen to increase the complexity of classroom management tasks, by extending the range of ability and pace with which the teacher has to cope and by making additional demands upon the teacher's scarce time. In addition, the teacher may feel that s/he does not possess the requisite expertise to help with the understanding of a difficult concept or with poor spelling or reading skills. Then where such expertise is available, there can be concern about giving 'special' or extra help lest the pupils are stigmatised or 'shown up', or other pupils are denied the attention they also need. Teachers thus seem to be caught between the 'ideal' of giving pupils appropriate, individual help, and treating all in an equal fashion, and are further caught between the 'ideal' pedagogy of individual teaching and learning and the practical constraints of having to teach a large number of individuals at any one time, constraints which tend to lead teachers to plan their lessons for the pace and levels of understanding of the majority.

Such problems were seen to be particularly pertinent to the teaching of mixed ability groups, where the range of ability and pace of progress was seen to be greatest and demands on teacher time and pedagogy thus particularly acute. However, other forms of grouping were not always regarded as solutions to management problems. Teaching a streamed, banded or setted group, where abilities and pacing might be more homogenous, was also perceived to generate certain difficulties. Such grouping might allow the teacher to 'pitch' the work more appropriately but there still remained the question of teacher time. As one mathematics teacher, for example, commented, where pupils with learning difficulties are concentrated in one group,

> they all want your attention at the same time. And if you have twenty in the bottom set or even not more than fifteen, there is no way you can deal with fifteen or twenty at the same time which is what they all want. They just want someone to sit next to them and say 'If you can do that, then go onto the next one' and so help their confidence. But as soon as you leave them, they can't do it. This is one of the reasons we have two members of staff on the bottom set.

Other teachers also made the comment that to group pupils with learning difficulties together could increase the number of behaviour problems in such a class, since pupils with learning difficulties were not always highly motivated. Thus apparent solutions to the range of ability and pacing in the mixed ability class were seen to generate equal, though different, difficulties for the teacher.

What is particularly important about such perceived management problems is not only their implications for the choice of pedagogical strategies used by teachers (and in consequence their possible implications for collaborative work between remedial and subject teacher) but also the further insights thus offered into subject teachers' constructs and perceptions of learning difficulties. It has already been suggested that such constructs are in part related to the skills, content and pedagogy of particular subjects. It can also be argued that they are also meshed with the teachers' more general pedagogic concerns, namely the management of the classroom to facilitate the learning which then takes place in particular subjects. For example, the issues of 'ability' and 'pacing' are crucial to the management of teaching and learning, given that teachers have to 'sort out' their pupils to assess the stage of learning at which they are at, and then plan further to cope with the diversity of individuals and groups. The 'ability' and the pace of learning presented by the pupil with learning difficulties are important facets of this sorting and planning process because of the implications they have for successful classroom management. Terms such as 'slow learner' or 'less able' thus have a significance beyond their use as simple explanations for learning failure or as simple stereotypes of what is 'wrong' with such pupils. They are also sustained by the demands of the teacher's tasks. This perhaps partly explains why teachers may continue to use and think in terms such as 'less able' or 'more able' in a mixed ability setting, which apparently should be concerned with individual ability and achievement and why despite efforts to change the terminology of learning difficulties, on the grounds that ability, for example, is no longer considered to be the major factor in learning difficulties, terms such as 'less able' are still widely used[4].

Just as the dimensions of subjects teachers' constructs of pupils with learning difficulties can be used to illustrate the argument that such learning difficulties are not merely an individual, 'pupil deficit' question, but in part a 'social construction', so it can be suggested that the relationship of such constructs to pedagogical issues of classroom management provides another example of the grounding of such constructs in socially based definitions and social context. Perceptions of pupils' ability (or rather, lack of it) or their 'slow pace' may have as much to do with the way teaching is organised as with any intrinsic pupil characteristics. At the least, such characteristics may be exacerbated or ameliorated by the particular style of pedagogy and classroom management. It was interesting to note, for example, that those teachers who operated an individuated or individualised[5] pedagogy were less inclined to discuss 'slowness' or regard this as a significant learning problem. This may be due to the possibility that individuated or individualised learning, where pupils proceed at their own pace, does not generate the same problems of having to cope with 'slow' pupils as does whole class teaching, where slowness could impede the progress of the whole group and upset the planning and completion of lessons. On the other hand, such pupils were sometimes seen to need more time and attention, the consequence perhaps of independent working. With such an organisation of teaching, there were also other perceived difficulties, such as pupils not being able to follow instructions and obtain information from a worksheet or text, due to a low level of literacy skills. This is perhaps not surprising given that such an approach to teaching often puts a high premium on literacy, to read worksheets or other resources (Edwards and Furlong,1978, Evans,1985).

Evans (ibid.) also makes the point that the 'mode of transmission' of knowledge has a bearing on the cognitive and other attributes that are pre-requisite to successful learning. Thus whole class teaching, for example, with its use of oral instruction and which is based on assumptions that all pupils are listening when the teacher is talking and that talk is an adequate instructional mode, requires the skills of listening, attention and retention. Pupils who do not understand are seen to have failed to listen or pay attention. Where learning is more individual, on the other hand, the perceived problem may be 'lack of independence', lack of the skills, motivation, confidence and application required to work on one's own. In looking therefore at the perceived characteristics of pupils with learning difficulties, it is important to consider whether particular 'modes of

transmission', certain teaching approaches, may
require or be perceived to require certain pupil
characteristics and will thus influence constructs
of learning difficulties.
Thus different teaching approaches and
different subjects may foster very different
requirements from pupils. At the same time there
may be some common demands made of pupils. It was
suggested earlier, when looking at issues such as
basic skills and intellectual abilities, that the
apparently universal concern with such issues may
reflect their universal importance to subject
learning. Equally, given that teachers and pupils
normally work in large teaching groups, certain
characteristics and behaviours may be required which
are conducive to learning in such situations,
irrespective of the particular 'mode of
transmission'. Concentration, paying attention and
being motivated and well behaved may thus be
important not only in respect to particular subjects
and teaching approaches but because if pupils do not
possess these characteristics, the management of any
large teaching group may become problematic. In
particular, 'discipline' and 'order' will then
become an important issue, which may explain why the
behaviour of pupils with learning difficulties is
often a cause for concern. Certainly as Evans
(ibid.,p.11) has commented, we need to know more
about what it means to be able or otherwise in
schools and recognise that the issue of ability may
be more complex than is often realised. Some other
aspects of subject teaching, namely identification
and assessment, will now be discussed.

THE IDENTIFICATION AND ASSESSMENT OF PUPILS WITH
LEARNING DIFFICULTIES

So far it has been suggested that the criteria which
teachers use to assess or typify a pupil as having
learning difficulties reflect a concern with basic
skills attainments, with intellectual ability and
with various learning behaviours and
characteristics. It has also been argued that
constructs of learning difficulties are in part
related to the particular demands of subjects, to
the comparative performance of peers and to
influential perceptions of 'typical' characteristics
or behaviour associated with learning difficulties.
In addition, judgements of pupil performance may be
further influenced by factors such as the school

catchment area or by the pedagogical and management problems faced by the teacher in the classroom.

Such a model implies that teachers may spend a considerable amount of time assessing individual learning difficulties within the context of their particular subject, classroom and school and that typification of pupils with learning difficulties is thus quite a complex process, involving a lot of observation and making of judgements over the time it takes to get to know such pupils.

My research suggests that there may be a number of stages to this process. The teachers seemed to start by gaining 'first impressions' of a class, to establish a preliminary 'mapping' of who and who may not have learning difficulties. A number of 'pointers' or 'indicators' may be used in this process. For example, when asked how he identified pupils with learning difficulties in a class, a history teacher explained as follows:

> All sorts of ways. The obvious one is through the written work. Through the written work you get a sense of the level of understanding. There are those who are quite bright orally who just cannot express their thoughts and reactions to concepts through writing, there are a lot of other kids who have not got the vocabulary to deal with what is going on in the class, they are identified through a lack of interest, or possibly deviant behaviour is the first clue. Some kids are able to write and produce a lot of work but it is obvious they have not understood. So there are three perhaps different ways of identifying, also just a lack of work.

A science teacher suggested that

> inability to follow fairly simple instructions would be the most obvious thing, a lot of science is following a recipe and not being able to do that is one of the first signs. Problem-solving as well, when it goes off the direct line, deduce something from what you have done or someone else has done, inability to do that

and a mathematics teacher suggested he would notice

> lack of confidence. And then obviously, with an individualised learning scheme it does not

take you long to pick out those with reading problems. And that has got to be a learning difficulty, if there is a scheme which requires you to read and you can't. Possibly attitude, not necessarily to the subject but to the school itself. You get children, you can tell very early, who seem to have switched off and they must have switched off for a reason. It is difficult to say really. Sometimes it will come from the results they get at the end of the day or the questions they ask, if they ask, and it is the type of questions you get and the response you get as you try and help them through it.

Such impressions may be gathered on a fairly 'ad hoc' basis as the teacher begins to get to know pupils, marks the first piece or two of work or answers questions during the course of the lesson. Or such impressions may be more systematically collected, as described by a geography teacher:

The first thing I do when they come in is write on the board the list of the department's rules, to set some standards for the rest of the year but it also gives me an idea how well they can read what I have written and how well they write it down. That is the first thing. Then I look at the first piece of work they do, you can nearly always tell, how they form their letters, writing in capitals and doing proper joined up writing and so on. And then following that we have a lesson ... reading it out from the worksheet and you go round the class, asking kids to read bits out, how well they cope or otherwise. Sometimes the copying off the board, I extend that to a bit of dictation, it should be theoretically easy enough to copy stuff off the board but when they are hearing me speak it is a different kettle of fish. The whole week's work usually in the first week of term is geared towards how well they can read, write, follow simple instructions and you can usually get good ideas as to who can cope and who cannot.

Such 'first impressions' seem to perform a number of purposes. They may allow teachers to begin to work out a 'mapping' of the class, in terms of the level of skills, knowledge and attainments possessed by pupils. They may also help to indicate whether certain pupils may present behavioural difficulties. The 'pointers' used by teachers seem also to be concerned with 'functional competence', with the possession of those skills and attainments which are seen to be necessary to participation in learning in lessons or in a particular subject, such as being able to read, or follow instructions, or copy from the board. Such first impressions may thus indicate which pupils may not be able to 'cope' with the normal lesson, in terms of content and activities, and who may therefore need some modified work or additional attention. In a sense, the teacher is not only identifying those pupils who may not 'cope' but also those pupils with whom, too, the teacher will have to 'cope', by providing appropriate work or a different teaching approach. Functional competence as well as comparative performance in relation to other pupils in the class may be very important since the demands on teacher time and future planning may be very different in respect to the pupil who is, for example, unable to read or write, as opposed to the pupil whose progress is not at the same level as his or her peers but who can nevertheless work independently. And then gradually such 'first impressions' may be further verified or modified, as a teacher gets to know individual pupils, and the whole class, and can begin to establish whether problems may arise with subject content, or skills, or whether certain learning characteristics or abilities may inhibit learning and progress.

Such 'first impressions' may also be verified or modified by discussion with the remedial department. Interestingly, many of the teachers whom I interviewed preferred to make preliminary judgements about pupils for themselves, on the grounds that such a procedure could avoid pre-emptive 'labelling' and perhaps offer opportunities for a 'fresh start', particularly for pupils entering their first year of secondary schooling. Information from a remedial department could then be used to balance the teacher's own judgements. As one science teacher explained:

> We get information from K. (remedial teacher), a list, but what tends to happen, I put it in my bag, shut the bag, I don't think to get it out and say 'H'm, who is remedial?' I tend to look around, identify the problems myself, identify them first, in all the various categories in my mind and then I would consult

the list and see how it coincides. And usually it is not very different.

This approach thus differed from that of the remedial teachers I interviewed, who were concerned to identify, prior to intake, those pupils who might have learning difficulties. Thus they accumulated lists, information and test results from the primary schools before pupils arrived, adhering to the common practice in remedial work of 'screening' for pupils with learning difficulties. There was thus less concern with the avoidance of pre-emptive labelling or with the making of 'fresh starts': rather every effort seemed to be made to ensure that pupils who might need remedial help should be identified.

Why should some subject teachers wish to make their own judgements in this way? Perhaps subject teachers wish to make assessments of pupils which are more context-based than much of the information, based on general tests such as reading tests, which is offered by remedial teachers. Independent assessment also preserves some of the autonomy of the subject teacher. This is not to suggest that there is necessarily any opposition to the expertise and advice of the remedial teacher - indeed remedial teachers' assessments of pupils are used to confirm the subject teachers' own judgements and in some cases were requested immediately on meeting a new class. But the making of independent judgements does offer some control over definitions of academic performance and of learning difficulties. It is also perhaps important to recognise what may be a genuine concern about pre-emptive labelling. Paradoxically however, where judgements are apparently made on observed performance and characteristics rather than pre-emptive information, they may acquire a greater legitimacy since they can be justified in terms of 'evidence' rather than being seen as a consequence of possible stereotyping. This legitimacy may thus also be an important factor in teachers' concern to make their own judgements on some evidential basis.

However pupils' opportunities for the making of 'fresh starts' do seem to decrease. Although the teachers I interviewed referred to procedures of identification and assessment in relation to all classes new to them, they particularly mentioned the new intake when describing the use of independent, 'fresh' judgements. As pupils move through a school, more information about them does become available to teachers, which can limit the viability of avoiding pre-emptive assessment. Judgements may be passed from teacher to teacher and be drawn upon when meeting new classes. Department records, previous work and brief periods of former contact (when taking a substitution lesson for example) may provide pre-emptive information. Pupils being helped by remedial teachers may be seen regularly in that department and thus be identified as having learning difficulties, and informal conversation in the staffroom may call attention to certain pupils. Thus teachers may rely less on making their own judgements as information accumulates during a pupil's school career and they become 'known' as having learning difficulties. The need to typify pupils may also vary according to the grouping arrangements made within the school. Research has suggested that when pupils are pre-selected into streams or bands, teachers may well derive or 'take' assumptions about pupils from the grouping to which they are allocated rather than 'making' evaluations of their own about performance or characteristics. (Keddie, 1971, Ball, 1981). Mixed ability grouping, on the other hand, may encourage the 'making' of judgements since teachers cannot draw so easily on stereotypes. Perhaps, unlike the streamed, banded or setted group, mixed ability grouping may offer some opportunities for pupils with learning difficulties to more easily 'renegotiate' their identity with a new teacher, at least if they are not already too well known.

Whether preliminary judgements are drawn from the teacher's own observations, from information provided by a remedial department or from pupil grouping arrangements, they are likely to then be subject to some modification as knowledge about a pupil develops. It is at this stage perhaps that the subject-specific dimensions of pupils' learning difficulties will become apparent to the teacher, as the pupil is presented with the range of skills and knowledge pertinent to the learning of particular subjects. The teacher will also accrue more information about the pupils' particular learning characteristics and behaviour, for example that the pupil consistently has problems with concentration or retention or is poorly motivated. The pedagogical and management problems presented by the pupil are also likely to be more fully elaborated as a range of teaching strategies is deployed and characteristics such as 'slowness' may thus be imputed to the pupil. It could be suggested

therefore that the process of typification of pupils
with learning difficulties may be a mixture of
processes. Such typification may involve different
stages, analogous to those identified by Hargreaves,
Hestor and Mellor (1975) in relation to the
typification of deviant behaviour, namely the stages
of 'speculation', of 'elaboration' and then of
'stabilisation' as the pupil's 'identity' is
confirmed. On the other hand, some typification may
comprise a process of 'matching' pupil performance
with what is already known or with stereotypical
assumptions about such pupils, in a way which
remains somewhat speculative rather than elaborated.
As Woods has commented, given the numbers of pupils
in a secondary school with whom the teacher is
involved, it would be impossible for a teacher to
know all pupils equally well and have the time and
knowledge to engage in elaborate processes of
typing. Static, stereotypical typing may thus be
the dominant pattern, except perhaps in special
cases. (1979,p.176,1983,p.50). What is less clear
is whether pupils with learning difficulties are
usually such 'special cases', and thus subject to a
complex and detailed process of typing or whether
many of such pupils are primarily identified by a
brief and somewhat speculative matching with certain
stereotypes. We would therefore seem to need to
know much more about this aspect of subject
teaching, including the influence or otherwise of
information from remedial departments. Such issues
are not only of academic importance. Such
typification, if a somewhat summary process, may
lead to inaccurate assessments of pupils'
difficulties. It also has a number of consequences
for the pupil, in terms of 'identity' and the
teaching methods and approaches which may then be
deployed. This final aspect of subject teaching
will now be considered.

TEACHING METHODS AND STRATEGIES

Many methods and strategies for the teaching of
pupils with learning difficulties in subject areas
have been suggested. Such suggestions seem largely
to focus on two main aspects of such teaching,
namely the modification of content and presentation
to take into account literacy and other difficulties
and the organisation of teaching and learning for
such pupils in large, often mixed ability, groups.
Thus to improve the teaching of mathematics,

Larcombe (1985) has suggested that the key role of
the teacher should change from presenting
mathematics teaching to promoting mathematics
learning, ensuring a correct match of the work to
the pupil, a wide variety of topics and approaches,
the use of investigative work, the provision of
self-instructional materials and the development of
individual programmes of assessment. Duncan (1978)
considers that pacing is the key to teaching the
'slow learner' and Bailey (1979) offers a number of
approaches to learning difficulties in mathematics,
including the teaching of difficult vocabulary
before discussion, use of oral presentation and
tapes, encouragement of the use of pictures, graphs
and diagrams to facilitate thinking in concrete
form, the provision of practical work and apparatus
and the development of talk and verbal explanation
by pupils. Practical work, games and activities and
investigative problem solving are also recommended
by Dyson (1983) and by Williams (1985) who discusses
the development of problem solving strategies
through inter-related and overlapping stages.
Individual attention and the use of small groups are
recommended by Knights (1974) and Choat (1974), and
Larcombe (1978) reviews the different categories of
work schemes and makes suggestions about the
presentation of teaching materials, including the
importance of minimising verbal expression, of using
clear diagrams, of giving specific instructions and
ensuring that the conceptual steps are sufficiently
small. Bailey (1982) reviews the suggestions which
have been made about the minimum level of
mathematical skills needed in ordinary life and
which might comprise the basic topics taught to
'less able' pupils (see also DES,1982) and Denvir et
al (1982), reporting on the Schools Council project
on low attainers in mathematics discuss, amongst
other things, the advantages and disadvantages of
different types of pupil grouping and recommend the
development of a policy for such low attainers in
respect to mathematics teaching.
    The teaching of the 'basic subjects' of English
and mathematics is of course also widely dealt with
in books on remedial teaching and approaches to the
'slow learner' (e.g. Bell,1970, Williams,1970,
Westwood,1975, Griffin, 1978) and which stress the
importance of diagnosis, of individual work, of
carefully graduated programmes of learning and of
concrete, practical experience. The development of
language and literacy skills is also a major focus
of all English teaching (e.g. Adams and Pearce,1974)

although writers such as Stratta (1965) and Holbrook
(1968) have looked more specifically at the teaching
of English to pupils who have difficulties and argue
the importance of developing creative expression
through oral discussion and stimulating themes.
Jones (1972) and Raleigh (1978) discuss the problems
of mixed ability teaching and recommend a variety of
approaches and organisation, including class
teaching, group and individual work.

     In respect to the teaching of history to pupils
with learning difficulties, Langman (1978)
recommends the use of family and local history to
introduce documentation as a source of historical
evidence and to develop the skills of detection and
interpretation. Hallam (1982) suggests that work
should be related as closely as possible to what is
known of pupils' developmental levels and Wilson
(1982a,b) advises a reduction in the concentration
of facts and concepts, use of narrative style in
reading material to make it easier and the
production of small, manageable units of learning.
He also suggests that pupils should be encouraged to
use a variety of styles of expression when writing
and recording work and that they should be helped to
develop reading ability and research skills. Hull
(1980), discussing the preparation of instructional
materials, suggests that the density of writing
should be reduced, with a high ratio of pictures to
print, clear instructions, no complex sentences, the
use of short words and avoidance of the passive
tense. In looking at mixed ability teaching
(Hull,1978) he recommends the use of graded
worksheets. Hagerty and Hill (1981) also discuss
the simplification of teaching materials and
recommend the use of teaching machines whilst McIver
(1982), as well as looking at materials, and
recommending that attention be paid to readability
and to allowing the least onerous methods of
recording, also offers suggestions on local history,
history trails, audio-visual aids and syllabus
planning.

     In respect to geography, Williams (1982)
recommends the sequential structuring of exercises
to develop graphicacy and the use of 'geographical
talk' to assist pupils to give expression to their
thoughts. Hodkinson (1977) argues that topics with
a high interest potential should be used, that work
should be presented simply, with explanation of
technical terms and lessons should be structured so
that within the mixed ability group each pupil can
work at his or her own level, using worksheets and

open ended tasks. Kemp (1981) also recommends the use of progressive or differentiated tasks in mixed ability teaching and suggests that for less able pupils (Kemp,1979) it is important to use concrete examples, visual aids, practical tasks and work which is broken up into limited objectives. Cooper-Maggs, Hardie and Kirby (1983) recommend puzzles, games and graded work and Booth (1980) the avoidance of prolonged teacher talk, the use of plenty of non-writing activities, map work and field work, simulation and role play. Catling (1984) suggests that mapping activities and skills should be carefully sequenced. A collection of articles on the teaching of 'slow learners' through geography (Corney and Rawling,1985) gives advice on the use of role play, simulation, computer assisted learning, drama and creative work. Practical activities and games are recommended for map work and worksheets should provide a range of activities, not just reading and writing, with care taken to simplify geographical ideas. Arkell and Haley (1978) recommend the use of audio-visual aids, teaching machines and tapes and Ciesla (1979) a modular structure of course design.

Modular courses are also recommended for the teaching of science by both Clegg and Morley (1980) and Kershaw and Scott (1975). Sturges (1973) suggests that worksheets and a circus of experiments are appropriate to unstreamed groups. Senior (1979) argues the value of concrete experience and Nettleship (1972) recommends the use of practical worksheets rather than traditional written work and recording. Hinson (1982) stresses the importance of helping pupils to acquire scientific vocabulary and of recognising that less able pupils are often at the stage of concrete operational thinking. Teaching materials should thus be critically assessed and cooperation between remedial and science teachers be developed to plan courses and adapt materials. For modern languages teaching with pupils who have difficulties, Smith (1973) recommends the development of basic phrases and dialogue and the use of background studies. Buckby (1979) argues for the use of graded objectives and tests and the replacement of work on structures with work on notions, functions and situations. Murray (1980) suggests the development of survival language competence, of conversation and of background information and Lewis (1973) the use of objects, pictures, puppets and games.

This necessarily brief review of the many

suggestions and strategies contained in the literature on subject teaching for pupils with learning difficulties does nevertheless indicate what sort of approaches are being mooted. The modification of content and presentation may include minimising the amount of reading and written work demanded in worksheets, using pictures, graphs and diagrams and the simplification of facts, ideas and concepts. Knowledge may be presented in small, graduated units which take account of pupils' developmental stage and their interests and abilities. Alternative modes of presentation to written text, such as audio-visual aids, teaching machines and oral discussion are recommended, as are practical activities and learning from concrete experience. In respect to the organisation of teaching and learning, combinations of individual, group and class work are suggested, with strategies such as graduated and open-ended worksheets and activities being used to overcome the problems of differing abilities and pace of progress within the class. A major theme concerns the importance of providing for 'individual needs' and ensuring that work is appropriate for the level of development, skills and knowledge held by such pupils.

The subject teachers whom I interviewed in my research also put forward some of the approaches they had developed to teach pupils with learning difficulties. Some had developed programmes of individual, resource-based learning, so that pupils could work at their own level and their own pace. Others had incorporated group work into the lesson pattern, so that different groups could proceed with different work at different paces. Others maintained an overall pattern of class teaching but within that pattern, the learning experiences of pupils with learning difficulties might be differentiated according to 'pace' or 'content'. A geography teacher, for example explained that

> the better kids do all of the topic and the poorer kids do as much as they can manage in the same time as the better kids. Like this worksheet on weather, there are three tasks and it will take the poorer kids all the time to do the graph of the climate whereas the better kids will do the graph, the description and the comparison in more or less the same time.

A history teacher described a different approach, of giving different work to different pupils or providing extra attention:

> I aim for the middle and then go over and speak
> to them (pupils with learning difficulties)
> separately. I have a piece of work that
> everyone can do and then go out from there,
> sometimes a piece of work for the slower ones
> of a simpler type and more difficult work for
> the brighter. And then it is just a question
> of setting up your resources for that.

Where different work, or a common starting point for
all pupils, including those with learning
difficulties, was provided, attempts would be made
to simplify language, to avoid too much reading or
written work, to provide pictures and diagrams,
explain vocabulary and offer some practical
activities. Care would also be taken in oral
presentation by the teacher to use simple language,
explain vocabulary and concepts and provide concrete
and familiar examples as illustration.
   Nevertheless all of these many suggestions
about the teaching of pupils with learning
difficulties in subject lessons are not without
accompanying problems. For example, as one science
teacher commented about a course using individual
resource-based learning,

> You have got very practical problems, getting
> out the equipment which we have minimised in
> the new course but still there are problems,
> kids saying 'Where are the test tubes' or 'I
> have broken this' etcetera, which can be
> annoying when you are sitting down with
> someone, working something through and you have
> to go off and sort that out, which can
> interrupt the flow. And then there are so many
> kids who have so many problems and they cannot
> get much help from each other in the individual
> situation.

Individual and group work can also be very stressful
for the teacher, as one modern languages teacher
explained:

> We have tried it, we devised our own course and
> I found that wearing. There were about four
> groups in the classroom who would get to the
> same point at different stages and I was having
> to explain 25 times or more than that because I
> would have to explain to some kid twice. And I

was coming out of that lesson really feeling
frustrated. Then they can work on their own
orally, working in pairs, that is alright,
because there is a general noise, but when it
comes to listening, you have got to have the
room silent.

The preparation of individual work or of a range of
work which included provision for pupils with
learning difficulties could also demand a major
commitment of time and resources, as a geography
teacher pointed out:

We have been to meetings and they all say to
pitch your lesson at the middle or the best or
do graded standards of worksheets, all this
sort of thing. It takes an awful lot of time
and expertise to get all this done, do it
properly. There are some schools which have
gone over to this sort of thing and if you look
at their resources area, it is huge, whole
trees of paper.

Such preparation, and the teaching required in
lessons, to deal with individual difficulties or
provide appropriate explanations, could also make
great demands on the teacher's expertise, an
expertise which did not necessarily include a lot of
knowledge about or experience of pupils' learning
difficulties.
    The teaching approaches and strategies
recommended and employed by subject teachers may
therefore have certain limitations. In addition, as
Williams has commented, in looking at the advice
offered by geography teachers, such advice tends to
consist of a 'series of strategies for coping',
strategies which focus upon

the teaching difficulties of teachers and how
to resolve these rather than upon the learning
difficulties of pupils and how these may be
reduced.
(1982,p.131)

Given the material conditions of teaching, such as
large classes and limited resources, it is not
surprising that 'coping strategies' should be an
important element of teachers' approaches to pupils
with learning difficulties. However such approaches
tend to be viewed as 'solutions' to pupils' 'needs'.
In many instances they may indeed effectively cater

for such 'needs', and it could be argued, somewhat in contrast to Williams' evaluation, that many suggested approaches do attempt to come to terms with the problems of catering for pupils with learning difficulties in large groups and do look in specific detail at individual problems and how to overcome them. However the possibility that such approaches are also addressed to the 'needs' of teachers has also to be seriously examined[6].

Such teaching approaches may also engender other problems. For example, although the modification of materials and methods may facilitate access to learning experiences and the achievement of 'success' as opposed to 'failure', there is the possibility that certain modifications could reinforce the very learning difficulties which pupils have or are perceived to have. At the simplest level, a reduction of reading and writing demands in instructional materials may reduce the opportunities which pupils have to practice and develop the very reading and writing skills with which they have difficulties. Moreover, to limit the difficulty of concepts, or reduce content or skills to be learned, or to see subjects as a medium for basic skills development rather than as learning in their own right, could prevent the very engagement with the 'essence' of a subject, whether this be creativity in English, hypothesising in science or understanding patterns and models in geography, which subject teachers do seem to define as a major feature of successful learning in subject lessons and which is seen to be lacking in pupils with learning difficulties. Thus unless such modifications are carried out with care, they may well increase differentiation between the 'successful learner' and the pupil with learning difficulties.

Equally the benefits of different approaches to the organisation of teaching and learning need to be carefully considered. Although class teaching may pose many problems in respect to the effective teaching of pupils with learning difficulties who may not understand the teacher's presentation or the work set or may be slow to complete work, individual, resource-based learning may bring with it some new problems, or certainly a reformulation of old ones in a different setting. Such a mode of teaching may make particular demands on literacy skills, the very skills which pupils with learning difficulties may not have. Whatever attempts may be made to reduce literacy demands (which in itself, as

just noted, may be counter-productive), written
information, on what to do and what is to be
learned, is likely to remain a major form of
communication, especially since the teacher's
capacity to cope orally with pupils' work and
questions may be even more limited than in class
teaching, since pupils are working individually and
cannot be spoken to as a group, one of the more
economical ways of allocating teacher time. In
addition, such organisation may require other
characteristics in addition to being literate, such
as the ability to work independently, which may be a
problem for certain pupils. Moreover, if there are
few opportunities for social, cooperative work,
pupils may experience isolation, an isolation which
is further compounded by the individualisation of
their problems and failures. Although the
differentiation of work according to pupil 'needs'
may seem to provide certain solutions to the range
of pace and ability found amongst pupils, and
'individual' approaches may allow pupils to proceed
at their own pace with appropriate work, it does
raise a number of difficulties.

The differentiation of the curriculum, through
individuated or individualised work, also raises
other problems. Not only may it unintentionally
'show up' the relative abilities and attainments of
pupils with learning difficulties (who at least in
other settings such as whole class teaching could
'pretend' understanding and perhaps not always be
seen as 'different'), but it may also result in the
continual reinforcement of the academic 'identity'
of pupils with learning difficulties. In
particular, the pupil may feel his or her identity
to be confirmed by individual work which is easier
or different, or by an inability to complete tasks
as quickly as other pupils. In addition, as Ball
(1980) notes in his discussion on the use of
worksheets in mixed ability lessons, the greater the
extent of individuation, the greater the possibility
of curricular differentiation (p.45). Some pupils
may always finish more work, others less, some
therefore covering all the syllabus and more, others
scarcely completing basic or 'core' topics. This in
itself may be problematic enough, in terms of the
different curricular experiences thus afforded to
pupils, but such differentiation may also have a
number of consequences for future 'careers' within
schools, particularly in relation to future
examination courses. Individual learning may even,
paradoxically enough, given the apparently

egalitarian import of mixed ability grouping in which such learning is often provided, operate as a more efficient mechanism of selection and differentiation than other methods such as class teaching, since it facilitates teaching to the differences between pupils and the emergence of different levels of attainments unrestricted by the common or 'average' levels of ability or pace of working which may dictate progress where the class is taught as a whole.

Approaches to the teaching of pupils with learning difficulties, particularly perhaps in the large, mainstream, mixed ability teaching group, thus raise a number of dilemmas. Work which is apparently appropriate to the 'needs' of the individual may paradoxically reinforce the very 'needs' it was designed to overcome and may also reinforce the 'special' identity of pupils to which it is given. At the same time, forms of teaching which make no allowance for individual difficulties are likely to generate and reinforce failure and do not recognise the unequal resources which pupils may bring to lessons. That inequality may then persist or indeed be exacerbated. Such problems and dilemmas are aggravated even further by the constraints of limited teacher time and resources and by large classes which restrict the time and attention which can be given to specific and individual difficulties. Certainly there are no easy answers and it may be possible to offer only some form of 'compromise' or 'coping' solution which at best addresses only part of the problem. That of course may be better than no solution at all, but in positing the value of any method or strategy, its limitations do need to be recognised, not least in respect to some unintended as well as intended possible consequences. Some of the implications of these approaches, together with some implications of other aspects of subject teaching which have been considered, will now be discussed in relation to the development of 'remedial education across the curriculum'.

SOME IMPLICATIONS FOR REMEDIAL EDUCATION

What then are the implications of some of these findings and issues for the theory and practice of remedial education? There would seem to be an urgent need for more knowledge about subject teachers' constructs of pupils with learning difficulties and more research on the skills, knowledge and characteristics required by pupils in different subjects and different 'modes of transmission'[7]. There is also an equal need for more knowledge about the processes of typification involving pupils with learning difficulties. Such research could further illuminate the issue of educability. Sociological debate on educability has largely focused on the pressing question of disparities between the educational attainments of pupils from different social class and ethnic backgrounds and accounts of the reasons for such disparities have variously imputed the causes to 'deficits' in the socio-cultural environment of certain pupils, to inadequate educational provision and practices, to structural inequalities in society and to the dominance of certain definitions of knowledge which may facilitate the educational progress of some pupils and impede that of others (Flude,1974). This sociological approach, which is now also particularly concerned with the processes of schooling, has however rarely been related to debates about educability in the field of remedial and special education, debates which have been dominated by categories of educability which are primarily psychological or medical in orientation and draw on individual rather than social explanations. If the curricular and the pedagogic aspects of academic 'success' or 'failure' were more clearly understood, this might facilitate further delineation and analysis of the complex inter-relationships between definitions of knowledge, the processes and functions of schooling, social inequalities and the pre-dispositions (perceived and actual) which may be related to class, race or gender and to individual capacities and experiences. Perhaps the redefinition of remedial education and new approaches to special education, which posit a new interface between special and mainstream education, will generate more awareness of the need for a broad and multi-faceted approach to the issue of educability, in which the tensions and the relationships between its individual and social dimensions could be explored[8].

There are also however some more immediate implications for remedial teaching. The traditional view of learning difficulties would seem to be unsatisfactory for a number of reasons. The identification of such pupils has frequently been based on general criteria such as intelligence or reading age, with little attempt being made to investigate the standards of literacy (or other basic skills) actually required in the classroom. Equally it would seem that despite their importance, little attention has been directed towards learning difficulties in particular subjects and towards the skills, knowledge and characteristics which may be required in particular subjects or types of lessons. If 'remedial education across the curriculum' is to be implemented and pupils' attainments be thus improved, remedial teachers will have to begin to look at such difficulties and requirements and draw up criteria for identification and assessment which more accurately and sensitively reflect the whole context of pupils' learning, rather than just relying on tests and other procedures which assess skills and abilities out of the context in which they will be applicable and needed

The new cross-curricular approach, in emphasising the need for curricular and organisational change in schools, implicitly repudiates at least some of the assumptions about 'pupil deficits' which have been characteristic of remedial education. However it needs to be more explicitly acknowledged that such 'deficits' have a social context and may be related to certain definitions of subject skills, content and pedagogy or certain styles of teaching and classroom management. This might encourage alternative interpretations or explanations of learning difficulties which pose the need for changes in schools and not just in pupils. The move away from a 'pupil deficit' approach may also have to be accompanied by assessment procedures which do not posit comparison with other pupils and thus do not define those who fail to reach certain 'norms' as somehow 'deficient' or less able or competent than their peers. Perhaps criterion-referenced assessment procedures could help to determine the requirements of pupils made across the curriculum and thus better identify those pupils who may then need some additional help or some modification of materials or teaching methods. Whether all comparison can be avoided is another matter, for as Croll, Moses and Wright have noted, if we are concerned to assess pupils, any criterion is 'only meaningful against the concept of what is appropriate for a child of that age or developmental stage or with that level of educational opportunity' (1984,p.147). Moreover schools are very much concerned with the comparative evaluation of pupils. Nevertheless the use of specific criteria in assessment may more easily relate that assessment to the contexts in which remedial help may be given and could perhaps reduce, to some extent, the dominance of concepts of 'normal' (and thus 'abnormal') performance found in schools.

The redefinition of remedial education also posits a 'preventive' approach to learning difficulties with the emphasis now put on curricular and organisational change. However if the primary orientation of such 'prevention' is laid on the importance of screening and monitoring pupils to discover learning difficulties, the wider preventive import may be lost in continuing assumptions that it is individual problems which are important and not those changes in schools. The new emphasis on 'individual needs' or 'special needs' is also somewhat problematic, for although it may make teachers more sensitive to those 'needs' and to the importance of change to accommodate them, it may also inhibit such change by posing problems and their solutions in individual terms which do not raise the wider issues. More consideration needs to be given to ways in which such 'individual needs', which are important, could be construed without implying they are the primary or only problem.

The issue of 'individual' or 'special' needs is also pertinent to the teaching strategies and methods which may be employed to teach such pupils. Many of these are predicated on such 'needs' and indeed provision for 'individual' or 'special' differences is now often seen as the hallmark of 'good practice' not only in relation to pupils with learning difficulties but all pupils. The value and the implications of such a definition of 'good practice' would however seem to need some further examination. If the constraints of teaching large groups, given current resources and staffing, will inevitably militate against the realisation of such practice, then it seems inappropriate to hold it up as the 'ideal model'. Not only may such a model foster a continued disjunction between 'theory' and 'practice', or mystify the extent to which teachers' as well as pupils' 'needs' may be served by certain teaching approaches and strategies, but if such approaches and strategies are perceived to be truly 'individual' or 'special' and still pupils do not learn successfully, there may be every inclination to impute such failure to the problems of pupils. Although such imputations hold wide credence even now, they are often tempered with a recognition that the limitations of time, expertise, staffing and lack of individual help may contribute to pupils' learning problems. The belief that 'needs' can and should be catered for given the present material conditions of teaching may just obscure the many issues involved and inhibit the very changes needed by pupils with learning difficulties.

The consideration of subject teaching with pupils with learning difficulties thus raises a number of issues and dilemmas which will need to be discussed by both remedial and subject teachers. A number of the issues which have been raised will need considerable research to facilitate the effective development of 'remedial education across the curriculum'. However such issues and dilemmas could also be a major focus of the 'new partnership' between remedial and subject teacher. Some aspects of this 'new partnership', how it may be realised and the problems which may be encountered, will now be discussed.

NOTES

1. Recognition is sometimes given to the difficulties or requirements of the subject as well as to the difficulties of pupils. However the problems of pupils are still seen in individual terms and such subject requirements are not themselves regarded as problematic.

2. See Chapter Five for some further discussion of pupils' perspectives.

3. This discussion of subject teachers' constructs of learning difficulties has focused on curricular aspects. There are, of course, a number of other issues which need to be considered, such as the influence of beliefs about the effects of home background, or about a particular school catchment area and the problems which its pupils will present, or about the relationship between certain characteristics (such as pupil behaviour) and learning difficulties, which may be held by teachers. There is also the question of teacher perspectives, including the norms and beliefs of particular subject sub-cultures and also more general perspectives in relation to the knowledge, skills and attainments which education should encourage and engender. This chapter is concerned with a review of subject teaching in order to delineate some of the issues involved in redefining remedial education. It is acknowledged that much more research and detailed consideration needs to be given to the problem of 'learning difficulties' and

to issues which have not been discussed here.

4. Teachers' continued use of pupil categories in mixed ability settings has been well documented (e.g. Ball,1981, Evans,1985). Apart from the pressures to differentiate which are generated by problems of managing large groups, the selective functions of schools need to be considered. Whilst comparison and selection remain important, it is unlikely that such categories will cease to be used whatever the type of pupil grouping involved.

5. Gough and McGhee (1977) suggest that a distinction should be made between 'individualised' learning, where pupils' work programmes are unique to them, and 'individuated' learning, where pupils work on similar programmes but by themselves and usually at their own pace. The majority of 'individual learning' falls into the latter category.

6. Including the recognition that 'coping strategies' are not only a matter of classroom management but may also be a part of the modification of learning materials. For example, it could be argued that the simplification of such materials is as important to the teacher as to the pupil, since such simplification may then allow a pupil to work independently and thus require less teacher time and attention.

7. Consideration would need to be given to all subjects across the curriculum, including aesthetic and 'practical' subjects, not just the 'academic' subjects discussed in this chapter. It would also be important to look at differences within subjects, for they are far from homogenous, and explore how different views of the same subject may or may not generate different concerns about learning difficulties.

8. At the least this could involve sociologists taking cognisance of neglected categories and theories of educability that are to be found in remedial/special education (cf.Carrier,1983), whilst remedial/special educators could consider an issue which is frequently neglected by them, namely that the majority of their pupils are working class and/or black. The relationship between special provision and social inequalities could then be explored.

Chapter Four

THE 'NEW PARTNERSHIP' BETWEEN REMEDIAL AND SUBJECT
TEACHERS

Although the redefinition of remedial education has
been mooted and developed by a number of people
involved with remedial education and has been
actively proselytised by NARE, it remains difficult
to establish the extent to which this redefinition
has been welcomed and accepted by the community of
remedial education as a whole. It is even more
difficult to ascertain the views of subject teachers
or discover the extent to which new approaches have
been implemented in practice, since so few research
findings are available. The HMI survey of secondary
education (DES,1979) found no examples of remedial
teachers working alongside the subject teacher in
the classroom and a more recent survey of provision
for 'slow learning and less successful pupils' in
secondary schools (DES,1984) commented that

> those designated as remedial teachers commonly
> worked very much on their own and in such
> cases, although other teachers valued what
> remedial work was being done, they were rarely
> aware of what was actually going on and how
> they might support it.
> (pp.30-31)

It was thus recommended that schools should give
more consideration to collaboration between remedial
and subject teachers (ibid.).

Reporting on a survey of members of NARE, Gains
and McNicholas (1981) suggested that there is
considerable interest in new approaches to remedial
education. Bailey (1981) however, found, from a
small survey of remedial teachers, a considerable
reluctance to adopt a wider remit, which reluctance
he ascribed to 'natural conservatism' or perhaps,
lack of expertise. A wider and more detailed survey

of provision for 'slow learners' (Clunies-Ross and Wimhurst,1983) explored the five aspects of the 'new' remedial teacher's role as outlined by NARE (1979) and defined as 'assessment', 'prescription', 'teaching/therapy', 'supportive' and 'liaison'. It was found that these five functions were exercised to varying degrees. The assessment and diagnosis of learning difficulties was central to the work of every remedial department and the prescriptive role was well developed at classroom level, in terms of provision of individual learning programmes for pupils receiving remedial help. Remedial teachers spent a large proportion of their time in teaching individuals or small groups and were involved in liaison with parents and other agencies. However although it was common to find two remedial teachers working together with groups of pupils, it was not common to find remedial staff supporting subject teachers in mainstream classes. Examples of such supportive work were only found in 21 out of the 791 schools surveyed and a brief for supporting all pupils experiencing learning difficulties across the ability range was very rare. The giving of advice to colleagues in subject departments was also quite limited, as was involvement in policy making at management level (Chapter Four).

From the evidence of such surveys it has to be suggested that a redefinition of remedial education has not as yet been widely implemented in schools. Clunies-Ross and Wimhurst (ibid.) put forward a number of explanations for this situation. They suggest, for example, that the name of the remedial department may be an important factor: where the remedial teacher was called a 'learning adviser' this seemed to lead to expectations that such staff would work outside the remedial department and across the curriculum, whereas traditional terms like 'remedial' did not generate such expectations. The organisation of remedial provision could also influence the development of collaboration in that where a system of withdrawal was deployed, rather than special classes, more liaison between remedial and subject teacher seemed to take place. The personality of the remedial teacher, a capacity to offer a sustained programme of advice and the status held in school (e.g. the scale posts allocated to remedial teachers) were also considered to be important, as was support from the headteacher for a new, more collaborative approach.

Other explanations could also be put forward. Smith (1982) for example, has suggested that the remedial teacher's capacity to allay staff anxiety may be crucial in respect to the adoption of a remedial teacher as consultant colleague. Moreover the consultant teacher should be prepared to listen properly and show confidence in the ability and competence of those seeking advice. Perhaps therefore, collaborative work has been impeded by poor communication and inter-personal skills. Or it may be a question of the specialist subject knowledge of the remedial teacher. Clark, Barr and McKee (1982) found from their study of eight Scottish secondary schools that two thirds of the subject teachers questioned were willing to have a remedial teacher in the classroom. However over a third of this number considered it was essential that the remedial teacher should have a qualification to teach the subject involved. Given that few remedial teachers would have such knowledge and qualifications across a number of subjects, this would seem to suggest that subject teachers may in some instances be reluctant to accept collaborative work from a non-specialist in their subject. Ferguson and Adams (1982), in another Scottish study, found that the development of team teaching was often seen to be highly problematic, with remedial teachers becoming 'teachers' aides' or 'faithful retainers', taking a minor role and helping individual pupils but rarely contributing to a full team teaching situation. The majority of teachers questioned in this study also considered that withdrawal was as effective as support in class. Problems of team teaching and the view that withdrawal is the most effective method of helping pupils with learning difficulties may thus be inhibiting the development of collaborative work.

When looking therefore at the implementation of redefined remedial education, it is important to be aware of a number of factors which may facilitate or militate against such a development. It may indeed be the case that the status and name of the remedial department, the organisation of provision, the support of the Headteacher or other institutional features are the most crucial. Equally, the views of subject teachers, their concern about specialist subject knowledge, their anxieties about requesting advice or their perceptions of what is the most effective form of remedial help, may influence the adoption or rejection of collaborative work. The views of remedial teachers themselves may be equally crucial - perhaps they are indeed reluctant to take on a wider, advisory role or work in the mainstream classroom or perhaps they would like to adopt a new approach but are unable to do so because of institutional impediments or discouraging responses from other colleagues. On the other hand, the main problems of implementation may be associated with the difficulties of establishing a team teaching situation or training remedial teachers to have the necessary skills and expertise.

Certainly a considerable programme of research would seem to be needed, to establish the extent to which any redefinition of remedial education is being accepted and how it is being implemented. Such research could look at the factors which have already been discussed. In addition it would seem important to examine the perceptions and interpretations of teachers involved. What, for example, do remedial and subject teachers mean when they talk of support for pupils with learning difficulties in the ordinary classroom and what views do they have on the advantages and disadvantages of such a new approach to remedial provision? Given that the issue of professional autonomy is an important component of teachers' occupational culture (Hargreaves,1980), why might subject teachers accept a remedial teacher working alongside them in their classrooms? If it is indeed the case, as Ball has suggested from his study of the implementation of mixed ability grouping, that

> a teacher's response to a proposed innovation and later his implementation of it, if accepted, are heavily dependent upon his commitment to professional and organisational norm reference-groups, particularly his subject department and subject sub-culture community, and upon the limitations of perceived constraints upon his practice, in terms both of collectively-held definitions of good practice and of the demands upon him as a 'producer' - that is, his perceptions of the demands made of him by super-ordinates within the school, his pupils and parents as clients, and the public community to achieve certain 'standards' or numbers of examination passes among the pupils he teaches
> (1981,p.287)

how will such commitments to professional and organisational groups and such perceived constraints influence the acceptance and implementation of redefined remedial education? And what strategies will be employed to protect those commitments and cope with those constraints?

The redefinition of remedial education and its implementation in schools thus raise a number of issues. Teachers' views about the value or otherwise of new approaches, their responses to collaborative work and the problem and constraints which may be encountered will be the focus of this and the next chapter. Such discussion will start with some consideration of subject teachers' views on the benefits of a redefinition of remedial education.

THE BENEFITS OF REDEFINING REMEDIAL EDUCATION

It has variously been suggested that the redefinition of remedial education could have a number of benefits for pupils with learning difficulties. A cross-curricular, supportive approach to provision could increase the long-term effectiveness of remedial work, provide greater opportunities for social integration, offset the stigmatisation that can accompany withdrawal or special classes, develop subject teachers' expertise and facilitate the adoption of 'whole school' policies, with comprehensive strategies for remedial help. The subject teachers whom I interviewed seemed to see many such advantages in this approach to remedial education. Integration, for example, with the pupils with learning difficulties being helped in the ordinary class, could overcome problems of labelling:

> If you take them (pupils with learning difficulties) out, the others can say he is a thickie and they get labelled. Whereas if they are in a classroom they are not getting labelled, not feeling different.
> (Mathematics teacher)

Academic as well as social arguments for avoiding withdrawal were also put forward:

> The basic problem why I do not like withdrawal is because that way you are labelling, saying this kid has all the problems in the book, get them out and give it to them from rock bottom. But you often find that some of the kids who have real difficulties with writing are more imaginative and the class misses out on their

imaginative input in any sort of work you are doing. They may not be able to write but may be the leader of the discussion work, so the class misses out and the kid misses out because there is a strength he is not able to show to the rest of the class.
(English teacher)

Giving support to pupils with learning difficulties in mainstream classes could also give such pupils access to the specialist knowledge of the subject teacher, as a science teacher explained:

There is a problem, a lot of people tend to think that the remedial department is a dustbin, they can't do this, they can't do that, I will put them in remedial. But having said that, I think a scientist should teach remedial children about science. Although they may have particular difficulties, they still want science, to do experiments, and they enjoy that, and I think that is best done by a scientist with cooperation from the remedial department.

(HB) Why?

Because of the scientist's expertise in his subject, he knows the ins and outs and there are ways to simplify it down, talk about the digestive system as a machine for example. Now someone who is not a scientist, who looks in a textbook and says 'I will do a bit on electricity today', their knowledge is not deep enough to make it simple, if you know what I mean.

However, despite such advantages, the teaching of pupils with learning difficulties in the ordinary classroom was also seen to create certain problems for such pupils. It was suggested, for example, that such pupils might not get enough individual attention and could not then benefit from the close personal relationships and attention afforded in the small remedial group. Where the remedial teacher gave support to such pupils in the ordinary classroom, this might give them the extra help they needed but could also thus 'point the finger' at their difficulties, identifying and stigmatising them as having problems. Among the teachers I interviewed there thus seemed to be a variety of views on the advantages and disadvantages of withdrawal or support in class and different evaluations of the benefits of these respective approaches to provision. This is perhaps not surprising given that the respective benefits of withdrawal and mainstream teaching have been much debated in terms of implications for effective learning, the meeting of pupils' needs and pupil-self esteem[1]. However from my research data at least, it would seem that subject teachers are willing to acknowledge the benefits which could accrue to pupils with learning difficulties from a more integrated, collaborative approach to remedial provision and would in many instances, accept the rationales and arguments for its implementation.

The subject teachers whom I interviewed however, seemed also to perceive and evaluate collaborative work and support for pupils with learning difficulties in mainstream classrooms in terms of the benefits which might accrue to teachers, as well as pupils. For example, a mathematics teacher suggested that such work and support might develop greater understanding between remedial and subject teacher in respect to their particular responsibilities and problems:

> It (collaborative work) keeps the remedial department not only in contact with the actual subject material but also the problems and difficulties of the teacher, that the teacher might be experiencing. I think one or two people have suggested that when they have contacted the remedial department, asking 'What can I do with this child?', some marvellous ideas have come up but they would involve you in about fifteen hours of preparation for that child. If nothing else, actually coming into the classroom would perhaps bring some of the idealists down to earth a little, they would actually see some of the problems which the class teacher has to face.

Support from the remedial teacher was also seen to provide some possible 'solutions' to the problems of teaching and classroom management which could be experienced, including the problem of the subject teachers' limited expertise, the difficulties of dealing with a range of ability and pacing and the limited amount of teacher time available.

Thus in respect to developing the subject teacher's expertise, a history teacher commented that

> S. (remedial teacher) has helped me a great
> deal in preparing work for these kids. I have
> had no training in this sort of work and until
> I taught in the mixed ability situation, I
> rarely dealt with the less able at all because
> where I taught before, the kids were withdrawn
> permanently into a remedial class. So I didn't
> really have experience of how to teach the
> really poor ones at all. There are so many
> ideas she has given me, advice on materials,
> the right things, and having the resources and
> knowledge to get stuff prepared. These history
> packages, we have done it between us and I
> couldn't have done it, known how to set about
> it without her help. She has taught me how to
> teach the less able.

The remedial teacher was also seen to support as
well as develop the pedagogical expertise of the
subject teacher through advice or support in class.
A science teacher, for example, suggested that the
remedial teacher was particularly able to appraise
teaching materials since

> he is able to look through, comment on
> readability and so on, more thoroughly than we
> could do that. We would expect to have a
> peripheral knowledge of these things, as
> teachers, obviously, but hopefully he has got
> his expertise from someone with experience,
> there might even be a bit of a research
> background, whereas ours will tend to be from
> our own experience. Also, he is dealing with
> those pupils a lot so he has the skills.

Such advisory work, of course, also provides
'reassurance' that the materials are right and thus
sets a 'stamp of approval' upon them, legitimated by
the remedial teacher's perceived special expertise,
(just as remedial assessment procedures may
legitimate the 'ordinary' judgement of the subject
teacher as to who has learning difficulties in the
class).
Advice given by remedial teachers on materials
or the presentation of the lesson was also seen to
help with the problem of 'pitching' the lesson to
cope with the range of ability within the class.
Support for pupils with learning difficulties
actually within the class could also help with this

same problem:

> Last year S. (remedial teacher) came in and was
> able to help me especially about this business
> of pitching it, she was able to give me a lot
> of tips and point out that what I was saying
> was going over their heads and by asking
> questions, she was able to bring things back
> down to basics.
> (History teacher)

> Even down in the second year there are certain
> pupils who founder ... in some cases it is nice
> to have someone like K. (remedial teacher) in
> the room with me, working alongside, watching
> and listening to what I am doing and then she
> is there to help, give guidance, translate down
> yet again to the pupils who are having
> problems.
> (Science teacher)

Similarly having a remedial teacher in the room
could assist with the problem of 'pacing'. With the
extra attention from a remedial teacher, pupils with
learning difficulties could make better progress,
not be held up by failing to understand something.
Such pupils could then be taught more easily along
with the rest of the group as discrepancies of pace
in completing work could be diminished. Having two
teachers could also mean greater opportunities for
group work, so that those with learning difficulties
could work at their own pace and not be hurried by,
or impede, the progress of others.

Support in class could also help with the
problem of 'time', as a geography teacher explained:

> You should be able to make sure the kids are
> doing the things you want them to, but no
> matter how hard you try, there is always
> someone who doesn't understand what you want or
> is doing it wrongly, nearly always someone who
> slips through the net ... and if there are two
> of you at it, you can minimise the number who
> make mistakes. It would also free me to give
> more time to the upper and middle levels of
> ability.

The problem of scarce teacher time is thus
alleviated in two ways. Firstly, with more than one
teacher, more time and attention can be given to
those with difficulties. Secondly, the class

teacher's time can be shared apparently more equably. Since those with learning difficulties are seen to take up a disproportionate amount of teacher time, because of their learning problems, having a support teacher to take some of the pressure off allows more time to be given to other pupils.

Collaborative work between remedial and subject teacher thus seems to bring a double benefit. It may help the pupils themselves, through the development of more appropriate materials and methods. Where the remedial teacher works alongside the subject teacher, giving help in the mainstream classroom, there may also be the benefits of academic and social integration and access to the subject teacher's particular subject expertise. In addition though, such collaborative work may help the subject teacher, provide support for and development of his or her expertise and offer solutions to the problems of 'pitching' and pacing and insufficient teacher time. In a sense, the 'new partnership' could be viewed as a new 'coping strategy' which might allow teachers to cope more readily and successfully with some of the problems of teaching and classroom management seen to be presented by pupils with learning difficulties.

If such an approach to remedial education is apparently seen to have so many advantages, why therefore has it not been widely implemented? It would not seem to be the case, from my research at least, that subject teachers would necessarily be reluctant to have a remedial teacher giving them advice or working alongside in the classroom. Or are there other disadvantages which have not yet been discussed? It was suggested, for example, at the beginning of this chapter that teachers' responses to an innovation might be influenced by commitments to certain professional and organisational norm reference-groups, in particular the subject department and subject sub-culture community (Ball,1981) and that teachers are also concerned with the issue of professional autonomy (Hargreaves,1980). It may be the case therefore that any 'new partnership' between remedial and subject teacher, whatever its apparent advantages, could impinge on such commitments and concern and thus render subject teachers less willing to collaborate. The possible influence of such aspects of subject teachers' views and responses will therefore now be examined.

COLLABORATION AND SUBJECT SUB-CULTURE

One way of examining the influence of subject sub-culture could be through consideration of the issue of subject expertise. It could be the case that subject teachers are concerned about the implications of working with a remedial teacher who is not a specialist in their particular subject. The study by Clark et al (1982) did find, for example, that of the teachers who were willing to have a remedial teacher in their classroom, a third considered such teachers should have specialist qualifications or knowledge in the subject concerned. In my own research few of the teachers considered that a remedial teacher needed to have such specialist subject knowledge: what mattered was the expertise in remedial work. Indeed it was sometimes considered an advantage to be a non-specialist in the subject concerned, for that might help remedial teachers to more fully understand the difficulties experienced by pupils. It was also suggested that since the level of work carried out by pupils with learning difficulties was not always particularly high, most remedial teachers would be able to cope. Where a remedial teacher lacked the knowledge to answer a particular question or relate a particular piece of work to the overall development of a topic, he or she could in any case always ask for help from the subject teacher. It was occasionally suggested that remedial teachers might have more difficulty with mathematics, science and modern languages than with other subjects, since these subjects did seem to require more background knowledge and had a rather more specialised vocabulary or needed particular skills, but most of the teachers in my research, including many teachers of science, mathematics and modern languages, seemed to consider that a remedial teacher's lack of specialist subject qualifications and knowledge was not a major barrier to collaborative work in subject teaching.

A desire to work only with other subject specialists would not therefore seem to always be a factor in subject teachers' responses to collaborative 'partnerships' with remedial teachers. Commitment to a subject sub-culture, to its specialised knowledge, may not necessarily result in reluctance to work with non-specialists. Perhaps the influence of subject sub-culture can be more clearly discerned in subject-based patterns of response to the redefinition of remedial education.

Certainly in respect to other innovations, such as mixed-ability grouping, there has been some evidence of such a pattern. A study by Reid, Clunies-Ross, Goacher and Vile (1981) found some quite marked variations in the response of different subject specialists to mixed ability teaching. Teaching approaches (e.g. the use of whole class teaching, small group work or individual learning) varied from subject to subject, as did perceptions of a subject's suitability for mixed ability teaching. Teachers of integrated humanities with or without an English component, for example, all considered this subject to be suitable, at least in some respects, for a mixed ability approach, whereas approximately half of the mathematics and modern languages teachers questioned considered mixed ability classes were not suitable (Chapter 6). In his study of the introduction of mixed ability grouping in a comprehensive school, Ball (op.cit.) found that members of the mathematics and languages departments were most resistant to the innovation and held to the view, traditional in these two subject sub-cultures, that the 'deep structure' of their subjects, their hierarchical or linear nature, made them unsuitable for mixed ability groups, at least without radical reduction in the level of academic work normally expected of the 'brighter' pupil (pp.179-80).

The study by Clark et al (op.cit.) of the views of teachers in some Scottish secondary schools found few significant subject-based patterns in respect to subject teachers' willingness to accept a remedial specialist in the classroom. The positive responses were spread across departments and it was considered therefore that response was unlikely to have been influenced by subject specialism, except in the case of subjects in whose classrooms a remedial specialist would not normally be placed (teachers teaching art and P.E. felt that the issue was not applicable to them) (p.36). Views on the desirability of extraction for remedial help, on the need for remedial teachers to have specialist qualifications and on the type of pupils who should receive remedial help also exhibited few subject-based patterns - responses varied both between and across subjects (pp.37-8). My own research is also somewhat inconclusive in respect to subject-based patterns of views on collaborative work and accounts of experience of advisory and team teaching work which have been written by remedial and subject teachers appear to give little indication as to possible variations in the success of such work with different subject departments[2]. Perhaps therefore the influence of a subject sub-culture may be less pervasive in respect to the redefinition of remedial education than it may be with other innovations.

Nevertheless there was some evidence in my research, of possible conflict arising from subject teachers' commitments to the norms of their subject sub-culture and community. Some English teachers, for example, suggested that a remedial teacher working alongside them would have to agree with the aims of their particular definition of English teaching. There was some concern that remedial teachers tended to focus on the mechanical aspects of literacy, that is the skills of reading and writing, rather than on the creative, expressive content valued by English teachers. There thus was some potential conflict between the two approaches and collaborative work would for them only be successful if the remedial teacher was willing to accept their approach. It was also suggested by some science teachers that the help given by a remedial teacher could upset the pedagogical plan of the lesson. Science lessons were seen to comprise a complex timetable of demonstration and experiments and if a remedial teacher took too long to explain or develop part of a lesson because he or she felt that pupils did not understand properly, this could impinge on the lesson plan and the completion of the lesson programme.

It may be the case therefore that where definitions of the appropriate content or pedagogy of a subject are potentially threatened by the contribution of a remedial teacher, conflict could arise. The advantages of collaborative work may then be balanced against the possibility that definitions of content and pedagogy may be questioned by the remedial teacher. Any 'new partnership' between remedial and subject teacher may not be welcomed if it is seen to undermine definitions of 'good practice' held by subject teachers. The degree to which this issue becomes a focus of concern from subject teachers may depend on a number of factors. In particular perhaps, much may depend on the extent to which the subject teacher strongly adheres to certain norms of the sub-culture in respect to what is defined as 'good practice': equally, of course, conflict may only arise if the remedial teacher is seen to have a different approach. Otherwise, even if definitions of 'good practice' are strongly held by a subject teacher, if the remedial teacher also agrees with such definitions, collaboration may not be problematic. Similarly, if the subject teacher is not too concerned about teaching a subject in a particular way, and a remedial teacher suggests a change in approach, agreement may well be reached without conflict. Much may also depend on the particular definition of content or pedagogy held by subject teachers. Not all teachers of English in my research, for example, raised the potential dichotomy between a skill-based and a 'creative' approach to English teaching. Nor did all science teachers raise questions about the effect on lesson planning which a remedial teacher might generate.

However, in certain instances, commitment to the norms of a subject sub-culture, to certain perceived definitions of 'good practice' in teaching a particular subject, may impinge on the development of any 'new partnership' between remedial and subject teacher. It was noted earlier in this chapter that a number of explanations for the apparent lack of such collaborative work in schools have been put forward. Many of these explanations focus on the institutional features of schools or on aspects of 'personal' interaction, such as communication skills or subject teacher anxiety. The inference from these explanations is that potential conflict may be overcome by effective listening, or by a 'diplomatic' approach to the giving of advice or by allaying anxiety at an inter-personal level. Alternatively collaborative work between remedial and subject teacher may be encouraged by changing the name of the remedial department or ensuring the support of the headteacher. Whilst such strategies may indeed be important, changes such as a new name or better inter-personal skills may not be sufficient to cope with potential differences of teaching approach between remedial and subject teacher, particularly where the subject teacher feels his or her commitment to particular definitions of the teaching of a subject are being threatened. What is also needed therefore is a particular sensitivity to subject teachers' perceptions of 'good practice' and to the influence of a subject sub-culture on such perceptions. Remedial teachers thus need to be far more aware of the dimensions of such definitions of 'good practice' and of areas of potential conflict with their own perceptions of 'what counts' as 'good' content and pedagogy[3]. The interaction between remedial and subject teacher presumed in the 'new partnership' could indeed perhaps be usefully characterised as interaction between different communities, each with their own perspectives, norms and collectively held definitions of 'good practice', who then have to try and negotiate some 'common territory'. Instances of 'territory defence' or 'boundary maintenance' between such communities could then be seen more clearly as not necessarily just a question of poor communication or personal anxiety but in some instances at least, as instances of conflict or potential conflict between possibly very different definitions of 'good practice'. It might then be possible to focus on what is the substantive issue of concern. Whether some common agreement can then be negotiated is another question, but at least the issues would then be clear.

ANXIETIES AND AUTONOMY

Nevertheless what might be termed the 'personal dimension' of interaction between remedial and subject teacher may be important. The teachers whom I interviewed in my research did talk about the need for remedial teachers to be 'diplomatic' in their comments and advice and felt that their confidence and competence should not be undermined. The inter-personal skills of the remedial teacher may thus be an important element in the development of successful collaborative work. Equally many subject teachers recognised that their own 'personality', for example, their willingness to accept constructive criticism, could contribute to the development or failure of collaborative work. However it is not just a question of inter-personal skills or 'personality'. What could be termed the inter-personal element of interaction between subject and remedial teacher is also embedded in the issue of professional autonomy and its importance within the occupational culture of teachers. It is also closely linked to the question of professional competence.

It is perhaps now almost a truism to say that the teacher's job is becoming increasingly difficult. The diffuse and multi-faceted nature of the teacher's role, demands for increased accountability, pressures to reform the curriculum, youth unemployment, changing pupil attitudes towards conformity and obedience, and financial stringencies, have variously contributed to the

stresses and problems of teaching and to a range of
anxieties about educational practice and
professional competence. Such changes have perhaps
brought such anxieties to the fore, but the issue of
competence has also a long standing within the
teaching profession. Teachers have often been
concerned about their personal competence, in
relation to discipline and academic results. Meshed
with this concern has been a wish for autonomy, not
just from the control of 'outsiders', such as
parents or the government, but as Hargreaves
(1980,p.142) has pointed out, autonomy from one
another in the classroom. This desire for autonomy
is tied in with the question of competence. As
Hargreaves goes on to comment:

> Like sexual activity, teaching is seen as an
> intimate act which is most effectively and
> properly conducted when shrouded in privacy.
> To be watched is to inhibit performance ...
> The heart of the matter, at the experiential
> level, is the teacher's fear of being judged
> and criticised.
> (ibid.,pp.141-2)

Autonomy thus protects anxieties about competence.
It also preserves the diversity of practice and the
opportunity to 'do your own thing', which is also
cherished by teachers.

Collaborative work with a remedial teacher,
whether it involves discussion of a pupil, requests
for advice on materials and methods or having the
remedial teacher actually in the classroom, could
impinge on such autonomy and create anxieties about
competence. And indeed, during my research some
teachers did make comments to the effect that with a
support teacher in the room you could not
necessarily be 'quite yourself' in your teaching or
relationships with pupils. There might be
inhibitions about 'having a laugh', or 'acting up'
to make a teaching point and relationships with
pupils were sometimes also seen to change. Some
teachers talked about the feeling, at least at
first, of being 'spied upon'. It was also suggested
that young teachers might be particularly
'threatened' by support work since they had not had
a chance to 'establish themselves', that is
establish their own particular and autonomous
approach to teaching. To accept such support
teachers had to be reasonably secure and confident
of their competence. As one history teacher

explained, for example, he was only too willing to have someone come in and help with materials and resources or comment on his teaching. However, as he went on to suggest,

> it is easy for me to say that though, I have been here quite a bit, I am quite secure, I think I am quite good, it is easy for me to say that. Trying to appreciate the feelings of someone who thinks they are not so good, insecure in their probationary year, in that situation ...

Certainly any partnership between remedial and subject teacher, particularly perhaps in the 'performance arena' of the classroom itself, has the potential to undermine the 'presentation of self' (Goffman,1959) as a competent teacher. Of course, although the classroom may well be a 'private domain', there are certain sources of information which can penetrate its insularity, for example the clues provided by examination results, staffroom gossip, pupil feed back and classroom noise (Denscombe,1980). However the involvement of a remedial teacher in a classroom or department may reveal substantial direct information on teaching performance, information, moreover, which is going to be assessed not only by another colleague per se but by an 'expert' in the field of learning difficulties, where the subject teacher may feel he or she lacks a similar expertise.

Thus it would not be surprising to find some subject teachers who were unhappy about collaborative work, nor indeed, remedial teachers reluctant to encroach upon the autonomy of other colleagues. Both the 'subject' and the 'personal' dimensions of professional autonomy need thus to be considered when looking at any 'partnership' of remedial and subject teacher. In addition though, it is perhaps also important to look at collectively held definitions of 'good practice' in respect to such autonomy. It has already been suggested that definitions of 'good practice' of a subject sub-culture may influence teachers' responses to collaborative work. More general definitions of 'good practice' in regard to autonomy and competence may be equally influential. If, for example, it is generally believed within a school that autonomy should be paramount and that 'good practice' or 'competence' involves the capacity to 'survive' individually within the classroom, without help or collaboration from colleagues, then support work from a remedial teacher may well be seen as a 'threat' and thus to be unacceptable. If on the other hand, cooperative or team teaching and open discussion of teaching problems is encouraged, then the rejection of support work may be seen in a different light. To want a closed classroom door under such circumstances is perhaps to suggest there is something to hide.

When looking therefore at responses to the redefinition of remedial education, in particular to the development of collaborative work between remedial and subject teacher, it is crucial to consider the range of perspectives, processes and explanations which may be involved. Factors such as the inter-personal skills of the remedial teacher may well be important but development of skills such as these may not necessarily be sufficient to overcome many of the pervasive influences of the subject and occupational culture of teachers. What is needed is a sensitive appreciation of the issues and social processes which may be involved in collaborative work, to find out 'what is really happening' when support work is accepted or rejected or problematic, and thus choose the most apppropriate strategies for change.

It could thus be suggested that the redefinition of remedial education provides another example of an innovation where a teacher's response, and consequent implementation if the innovation is accepted, are dependent upon commitment to professional and organisational norm reference-groups (Ball,op.cit.p.287). Much more research is needed, to examine subject teachers' perspectives and interpretations, the variations which might accrue from differences in subject content and pedagogy and in more general pedagogical perspectives and from different school contexts and definitions of 'good practice', and to examine the range of strategies which might be deployed to protect autonomy, subject boundaries and anxieties about competence. Such findings could then be further examined in the light of the demands and constraints upon teachers (cf.Ball,ibid.) and in the light of some of the institutional features of schools which have also been suggested as factors which might influence the implementation of a redefined remedial education. These last aspects will now be briefly discussed.

THE CONSTRAINTS AND THE CONTEXT OF COLLABORATION

What then are some of the demands and constraints upon teachers which could inhibit or facilitate the implementation of a new approach to remedial education? The teachers whom I interviewed in my research frequently suggested that one major constraint involved lack of teacher time. There were few opportunities during the working day to have discussion between remedial and subject teacher about individual pupils, or the development of new materials and methods. There were also few opportunities to discuss in any detail the management of any in-class support, which then sometimes led to problems of conflicting approaches in respect to the content and planning of the lesson or relationships with pupils (e.g. disciplinary matters).

A lack of sufficient remedial staff was also another perceived problem - with only one or two remedial teachers working in the school, support had to be spread thinly, which could lead to difficulties of organisation and relationships. For example, subject teachers might have only one lesson where the remedial teacher could provide in-class support for pupils with learning difficulties, and thus teaching strategies and approaches had continuously to vary. Pupils could develop expectations of teacher attention which could only be fulfilled when two teachers were present and such expectations then created problems when the support teacher was absent. Then, too, the remedial teachers had to be shared thinly across as well as within departments, so that they could only work with one or two teachers at a time in each department or with one department exclusively to the detriment of others. It was thus sometimes seen to be difficult to establish the close and continuous working relationship deemed to be necessary to a successful 'partnership'. Such staffing problems were further exacerbated by remedial teachers' commitments to basic literacy and numeracy tuition, which took up a part of the potential 'support' and 'advisory' timetable. It was not usually suggested however that these commitments should be decreased - most of the subject teachers I spoke to felt there was a need for such tuition for pupils with major learning difficulties - but such commitments still did bite in to the very limited remedial staffing available and thus impeded the development of cross-curricular and collaborative work.

Such material, situational constraints have their wider context, which was frequently recognised by the teachers in my research. Thus, for example, arguments for more staffing, to facilitate support and advisory work by remedial teachers were usually qualified with a somewhat rueful acknowledgement of the present climate of spending on education. A desire for more resources, lack of which was also perceived as major constraint on the effectiveness of provision for pupils with learning difficulties, was similarly broached with an acknowledgement that such resources were unlikely to be forthcoming. It was suggested that appropriate in-service training, to help subject teachers learn more about learning difficulties and about the teaching of their subject to pupils with such difficulties, could perhaps be provided with relatively less expense although major programmes of such training, especially at a school-based level, where they might be particularly effective, were seen to be unlikely to materialise.

It has been suggested that new approaches to remedial education and to special educational needs will in part be dependent upon changes in attitude and current practice. This may indeed be true and in some senses, the redefinition of remedial education is about changing current practice rather than about the expansion of staffing and resources. Nevertheless to ignore the very real constraints of current limitations of staffing, time, resources and in-service training is not only to do a disservice to teachers' understanding of those constraints but also to ignore what may be one of the most significant explanations for the current lack of extensive implementation of redefined remedial education. As will be shown in the next chapter, the remedial teachers whom I interviewed also identified such constraints as having a major impact on their capacity to develop advisory and supportive work. Notwithstanding all the other factors and processes which, it has been suggested, may influence the development of such work and which therefore need to be considered, the simple explanation that redefined remedial education has not been implemented because remedial and subject teachers do not have the time, staffing and resources to carry out such a development needs to be very seriously considered.

There is a further important element to the question of constraints and demands upon teachers. As suggested earlier in this chapter, subject teachers have to carry out a number of teaching and management tasks within the classroom and their efforts to provide appropriate materials or individual attention for pupils with learning difficulties are often perceived to be constrained by the limitations of teacher time and the problems of managing a wide range of ability and pace of progress in large teaching groups. Moreover such pupils are but one aspect of their responsibilities. Time and effort spent on such pupils has to be measured against demands on the teacher to 'produce' results with the 'majority' of pupils, both 'formally' (e.g. in terms of examination results) and in terms of the less formal but still very important requirements of producing work from pupils in the classroom which conforms to professional and subject definitions of 'good' learning and achievement. The pressure of such demands could be identified in worries about sharing out time and attention to all pupils, or 'covering the syllabus' and thus being concerned about the effect of a remedial teacher's involvement on the planning and completion of lessons.

It was suggested in the first chapter of this book that given the dominance of high-status academic knowledge within the secondary curriculum and given the attention and energy given to examinations and other teaching activities which often do not involve pupils with learning difficulties, such pupils are frequently relegated to a marginal position within schools. If teachers do not have the time to discuss materials and resources for pupils with learning difficulties and remedial staffing is limited so that opportunities to develop support and advisory work are thinly spread, then remedial teachers are unlikely to be able to put pupils with learning difficulties continuously 'on the agenda' and the marginality of such pupils to the main preoccupations of subject teachers may well continue. Even more importantly perhaps, whether sufficient time and staffing is available or not, if demands to 'produce' a particular kind of academic achievement and a high standard of academic results are still made upon subject teachers, then it is unlikely that any new approach to remedial education which involves the commitment, time and energy of subject as well as remedial teachers will be implemented. Subject teachers will continue to perceive themselves as being constrained (and indeed will be constrained) by other, more pressing demands which will thus impinge heavily on such innovation.

The question of such demands and constraints highlights the need therefore to consider the institutional and curricular framework and features of secondary schooling. It was mentioned earlier in this chapter that certain institutional features have been suggested as being relevant to the successful implementation of redefined remedial education. Clunies-Ross and Wimhurst (1983), for example, cited the importance of the name of a remedial department, the status accorded to teachers in charge of such provision and support from the headteacher. Such factors may well be relevant. A particular name or designation may well influence expectations and interpretations of the role of the remedial teacher. Issues like status and support from the headteacher raise the important problem of power. Remedial teachers have often been accorded low status and thus little power to change the curriculum or methods of teaching. If they enjoy a higher status and are supported by management staff, they may have more opportunities to persuade other teachers to adopt new approaches and might be able to effect greater change.

At the same time that power may be limited by other institutional and curricular features of the school. For example, the existence of very formal methods of differentiation between pupils, through streaming or banding, may tend to encourage distinctions between 'academic' and 'non-academic' pupils. It may then be difficult to ensure that teachers do not rely on stereotypical judgements about such 'non-academic' pupils or to encourage teachers not to think of such pupils as 'failures'. A curriculum which is strongly divided into 'subjects', or processes of curricular decision making which rely on the autonomous decisions of each subject department may reinforce differentiation between 'subject' and 'remedial' teaching and inhibit collaborative work and the development of 'whole school' policies. A staffing policy which gives little priority to remedial work may mean that little time or staffing is available to develop 'remedial education across the curriculum'. An 'ethos' which is competitive and stresses academic merit may create a very different climate for possible change from an ethos which stresses equal regard for all pupils, no matter what their attainments and abilities. Unfortunately, we still do not know precisely what makes a school 'effective', particularly for pupils of lower ability or attainment (Gray,1981, Reynolds,1985).

However it does seem to be clear that the 'climate' or 'ethos' and the institutional features of schools are important to its effectiveness and its 'results'. It thus would be reasonable to assume a similar importance in respect to the redefinition of remedial education. Some further research on the features of schools and their consequences for the redefinition of remedial education would be extremely useful, as would accounts by 'successful' innovators of new approaches which examined which features of schools seemed to constrain or facilitate such success.

The constraints and the context of implementing a redefinition of remedial education are of course linked to the wider features of the education system and of society and it may be the case that opportunities for changing certain school features or ameliorating certain constraints will be limited without more widespread change. It certainly seems unlikely, for example, that the constraints of time, resources and staffing are going to be remedied in the near future, given the present climate of restrictions on finance for education. However, it is perhaps worth noting that although these constraints, together with the demands made on the subject teacher to 'produce' good academic results, would seem to militate against work with remedial teachers, some of the constraints experienced by the subject teacher in respect to the organisation and management of learning may also afford a basis for establishing collaborative work. Teachers may well try to develop such work in any case, in the interests of pupils with learning difficulties, if they agree with its possible benefits. In addition though, their own interests may be served by such developments.

Pollard has suggested that one important facet of such interests 'relates directly to the self-image, identity and beliefs of the teacher' (1980,p.37). The constraints of teacher-pupil ratio and of managing a range of ability and pacing in a large group could be seen to set up a tension between the 'ideal' and the 'pragmatic', between what the teacher would like or feels ought to be done, and what can be done. This may then create problems of self-image and identity in that being a 'good teacher', if it is believed that involves, amongst other things, helping each pupil as needed, may not be possible in such circumstances. As Pollard notes, the issue then becomes

> the degree of maintenance of a particular self-image or belief compared with pragmatic adaptation to situational necessities. In a way it is a question of commitment to an ideal self or acceptance of a pragmatic self.
> (ibid.)

The teachers whom I interviewed were only too aware of the discrepancy between the 'ideal' and the 'pragmatic' in their teaching and of how the 'just' or 'fair' allocation of teacher time, for example, was a major difficulty. They were also aware that they were not always fulfilling the 'needs' of pupils with learning difficulties, because of lack of teacher time and sufficient expertise. The development of collaborative work between remedial and subject teacher would seem to offer some possibility of sustaining some 'ideal' notion about the effectiveness of teaching and classroom management. The 'pragmatic' self may thus be kept at bay, thus sustaining 'ideal' self-image, identity and beliefs. With a remedial teacher helping in the classroom, 'looking after' those with learning difficulties, or releasing time for the class teacher to pay them some attention, the allocation of teacher time could be perceived to be more just. The help which may be given with 'pitching' or 'pacing' the lesson may also help to maintain the belief that a diversity of pupils are being adequately catered for. Help with the development of the subject teacher's expertise or with materials and methods may also further sustain such beliefs and a self-image of being a 'good' teacher.

The 'new partnership' may thus offer two major benefits which could be seen to arise out of the many constraints faced by teachers. Firstly it may offer a concrete 'coping strategy' to help deal with the demands made on teachers in large groups by pupils with learning difficulties, since the remedial teacher can give his or her time, if giving support in class, to such pupils. Time and help may also be given with materials and methods to further aid the running of the lesson. Secondly such a 'partnership' may help to sustain the belief and the hope that the subject teacher's lesson is an example of 'good practice' where all pupils are given the help they need. Paradoxically perhaps, although a remedial teacher's involvement may at first seem to threaten 'professional competence' and certainly may generate anxieties about it, such involvement may actually help to support and sustain that competence, once collaboration has been accepted.

NEGOTIATIONS, STRATEGIES AND CONSEQUENCES

The 'new partnership' between remedial and subject teacher could thus be seen to have both advantages and disadvantages. It may offer certain benefits to pupils, such as social and academic integration with the mainstream of the school and improvements in teaching methods and materials as a consequence of the sharing of the remedial teacher's expertise. Pupils may also benefit from extra teacher attention in class if the remedial teacher is able to provide such support. Subject teachers may benefit too, from the 'coping strategies' afforded by such collaboration in terms of the development of expertise, and the help given to problems of 'time', or 'pitching' and 'pacing' work, and 'professional competence' and 'good practice' may thus be seen to be sustained. At the same time, pupils may lose some of the benefits of small groups and perhaps be 'shown up' in mainstream lessons when the remedial teacher gives them support or their work is modified, and benefits to teachers may have to be balanced against possible conflict over teaching approaches and against anxieties about professional autonomy.
     Certainly the development of such 'partnerships' is likely to involve negotiation between remedial and subject teacher, a process which may centre on perceived and actual benefits to pupils and teachers and on particular and possibly competing definitions of 'good practice' held by those involved. It thus cannot be assumed that if what remedial teachers offer is 'relevant' and 'practical', they will 'quickly win the confidence of their colleagues' (Lewis,1984,p.11) nor that if an innovation is intrinsically valuable and the innovator has the necessary expertise and lines of communication are efficient, then it will be adopted, as McNicholas has suggested in relation to new approaches to remedial education (1979,p.156). As MacDonald and Walker have commented, the assumption that we all have 'overlapping visions of curriculum excellence' may not necessarily be well founded and the most salient issue may be whether people actually want to hear what innovators have to say (1976,p.44). My own research would seem to suggest that subject teachers may welcome collaboration with remedial teachers and

thus may wish to hear what they have to say, partly due to agreement with some of the rationales which have been put forward for changes in remedial education and partly because of the benefits which collaboration may afford to them. However, such collaboration may not necessarily reflect the congruence of beliefs and approaches which 'partnership' seems to imply and the subject teacher, the other half of that 'partnership', may also have certain beliefs and concerns which may be different from those of the innovating remedial teacher. The outcome of any partnership may reflect the remedial teacher's 'agenda' of change but it may also reflect the subject teacher's various concerns, some of which may coincide with those of the remedial teacher, some of which may not.

There may also be 'hidden' agenda and strategies involved in such negotiation, for example, ensuring that the 'purchase' of the 'goods' of support, the 'coping strategies' afforded by collaboration, does not involve too high a 'price' in terms of less autonomy or conflict over teaching approaches. The outcome of such negotiations may thus depend on the degree to which a particular definition of subject content or pedagogy is strongly held, whether it conflicts with definitions held by remedial teachers, the actual pedagogical problems encountered in lessons and subjects and the status and power held by each of the 'partners'. It may also further depend on the inter-personal skills of the remedial teacher, on the degree to which there is pressure to produce good academic results, rather than cater for pupils with learning difficulties, on staffing and time available to develop collaboration and on definitions of what counts as 'good practice' within the school, in relation to team work and the role of the remedial teacher.

Such outcomes may therefore be different from those intended by remedial teachers, whatever the quality of their expertise or the values and benefits apparently afforded by new approaches to provision for pupils with learning difficulties. Moreover, although factors like the name of the department and the expectations it may then engender or the support of the headteacher may be important, because such 'partnerships' comprise interactions between members of different 'subject communities' within the school, each with their own concerns and definitions of 'good practice', such institutional factors are unlikely alone to determine the success

or otherwise of the negotiations involved in
collaboration. More attention could usefully be
directed towards the differences in definitions of
'good practice' between remedial and subject
teachers, how these may coincide or conflict in the
development of 'remedial education across the
curriculum' in various school contexts and how
negotiation takes place and certain outcomes are
reached.

What then may be the consequence of attempts to
redefine remedial education in secondary schools?
Given that this redefinition has not yet been widely
implemented and certainly has not been
systematically evaluated and researched, any
predictions have to be somewhat speculative. From
the research which is available, including my own,
and from accounts which have been written by
teachers about collaboration across the curriculum,
it would seem that new approaches may well be
welcomed by at least some subject teachers and the
'barriers' of lack of specialist subject knowledge
held by remedial teachers and of anxieties about
professional autonomy may not always be important or
may be minimised because of other benefits accruing
from a 'partnership' between remedial and subject
teacher.

However such a 'partnership' may well be
subject to a number of 'negotiations' between the
teachers concerned, resulting in a variety of
outcomes. Given the range of issues and practices
involved, there may thus be a considerable diversity
in respect to what constitutes such a 'partnership'
and what it may achieve in terms of the curricular
experiences offered to pupils with learning
difficulties. The remedial teacher may effect
certain curricular and organisational changes in
subject teaching but may also find that although the
value of the remedial teacher's help as an
additional 'coping strategy' for teachers may be
welcomed, the demands made on subject teachers to
'produce' academic results, the norms of subject
sub-cultures, concern about professional autonomy
and the material constraints of teaching may
militate against more radical alterations in
practice. Remedial and subject teacher may be able
to work together to minimise the effects of such
demands and constraints upon provision for pupils
with learning difficulties, but in some cases there
may well be conflict or the remedial teacher may be
no more than an 'aide', finding perhaps that
although the 'goods' of support are being provided,

the 'price', of sharing decisions or instituting change, is not being paid. Given the traditional low and marginal status of remedial teachers and the continued dominance of subject hierarchies, the latter outcome may well have to be expected, particularly if the constraints of not having enough remedial staff and time to develop close collaboration are not resolved. It will certainly take a lot of time and change to enhance the status and the power of remedial teachers to define situations on an equal par with subject teachers. Some of these changes, as they affect remedial teachers, will now be discussed in more detail.

NOTES

1. See, for example, Capron, Simon and Ward (1983), Kelly (1981).

2. Whether such differences were apparent and have simply not been recorded, or whether they did not exist, is however not clear. It would be useful if such accounts looked at such patterns of response and at the more general aspects and problems of working with subject teachers.

3. Conflicting and competing definitions of 'good practice' may be a consequence of different views about subject content, such as skill-based or 'creative' English, as discussed earlier. There may also be different views on the way in which such content should be presented and taught. In addition, the particular emphasis on an individual pedagogy within remedial education may be problematic in large classes, where the emphasis is on the teaching of a group, and the further emphasis within remedial education on teaching to 'individual need' and using curricular content to develop basic and other skills may conflict with views of subjects as having certain skills and knowledge which are intrinsically valuable and important, irrespective of pupil 'needs'. The meshing of the remedial teacher's expertise or 'good practice' with that of the subject teacher may therefore be a lot more problematic than has often been assumed, and may also be more diverse than sometimes postulated, given varying definitions of 'good practice' within subjects, or for that matter, within remedial education.

Chapter Five

REMEDIAL TEACHERS AND THEIR PUPILS

The redefinition of remedial education involves a considerable broadening of the traditional role of remedial teachers and a concomitant enhancement of their status. As overt rather than hidden sources of pedagogical expertise within the secondary school, remedial teachers will be 'change agents' charged with the improvement of provision for pupils with learning difficulties across the whole curriculum. It is also being suggested that this new remit should include a greater involvement with policy making at management level, to develop 'whole school' policies and strategies.

These mooted changes in remedial education appear to hold a number of benefits for pupils with learning difficulties. They will also, if implemented, change many of the learning experiences of such pupils. They are more likely to be taught in mainstream classes, receiving additional support from a remedial teacher. Materials and methods used for such pupils may well change as a consequence of the advice and support given by remedial teachers. In addition, though, redefinition of remedial education, if implemented, will also change the working situation of remedial teachers. They may spend more time in mainstream classes, working alongside the subject teacher, or be asked more frequently for help and advice. They may have to develop policies for both subject departments and the whole school. Such work may enhance their status but it will also make new demands on their expertise and time. What then may be the consequences of redefinition for remedial teachers and how may they themselves view such change?

It has sometimes been suggested that the adoption of a new cross-curricular role for remedial teachers should eventually result in the

122

disappearance of remedial provision as a separate entity within the school and indeed that the aim of work with subject teachers is to 'do away' with remedial teaching and teachers altogether. Galletley, for example, when arguing for a new approach, suggested that

> we must educate our colleagues ... We should proselytise far more actively, setting about achieving our own extinction. We are unique in that we should, by definition, have no permanent future.
> (1976,p.151)

McNicholas has similarly argued that remedial teachers should be 'striving for the cessation of remedial education as presently constituted', directing efforts towards 'prevention' rather than 'palliatives' (1976,p.115). If indeed such 'preventive work' was successful, there would be little demand for remedial teaching or for further support and advice from remedial teachers. If the remedial teacher's expertise is demystified and shared amongst subject teachers, as Lewis, for example has suggested it should be, in that

> remedial teachers must disclaim the myth that teaching pupils with special needs requires approaches, methods and techniques not available to or outside the repertoire of the subject teacher
> (1984,p.7)

it may well be the case that remedial teachers will 'disappear', their role having been taken over by other teachers, and with it, any specialist identity for the community of remedial education.

The 'abolition' of remedial education and the 'disappearance' of remedial teachers however presumes widespread changes in the organisation, curriculum and functions of secondary schooling. At present, even the implementation of redefined remedial education appears to be problematic, with few schools adopting collaborative work between remedial and subject teacher. It would seem more pertinent therefore to consider what changes are likely to take place within the current context and evaluate how redefinition is likely to immediately affect the community of remedial education, rather than speculating about its eventual demise. Three aspects of redefinition would seem to be important for remedial teachers. Firstly, how will the traditional concerns of remedial teachers mesh with the development of collaborative work across the curriculum and what changes in the traditional expertise of remedial teaching will be needed? Secondly what will be the possible consequences of the implementation of redefined remedial education for remedial teachers in respect to work demands, status, rewards and resource allocation? Finally, what opportunities or constraints will facilitate or inhibit changes in approaches to remedial provision? These inter-related issues will now be discussed.

REDEFINITION AND REMEDIAL TEACHERS

The redefinition of remedial education does involve some preservation of traditional areas of expertise and responsibility, such as the assessment of pupils with learning difficulties and individual or group tuition and counselling. However such traditional concerns are to be meshed with the development of collaborative work with subject teachers across the curriculum. This development raises a number of issues. For example, will the new aspects of remedial work minimise commitment to former concerns or will traditional responsibilities inhibit the implementation of cross-curricular work? The NARE Guidelines on the role of remedial teachers (NARE,1979) and on teaching roles for special educational needs (NARE,1985) continue to stress the importance of assessment and specialised tuition and counselling and accounts written by remedial teachers who have tried to implement new approaches still make reference to these aspects of the remedial teacher's role. It would seem therefore that the redefiniton of remedial education does not posit the abolition of such traditional concerns.

However there is a new focus on collaborative work and policy development. Thus the allocation of the remedial teacher's time, particularly in respect to time spent on assessment and specialised tuition, must necessarily change if collaborative 'partnerships' and school-wide policies are to be developed. In addition, such collaboration and policies may change perceptions of the remedial teacher's responsibilities and expertise, perhaps lessening the time spent on tuition and assessment or generating demands for new forms of expertise that have more to do with the teaching and management of large teaching groups than with individual remediation. To what degree and how, therefore, will traditional responsibilities and expertise have to change and how will this affect remedial teachers?

The remedial teachers whom I interviewed during my research had initiated various forms of collaborative work with subject teachers and were also involved in the support of pupils with learning difficulties in the mainstream classroom. However they considered that the assessment of pupils with learning difficulties, including the 'screening' of incoming pupils, was an important part of their responsibilities. They gathered information from primary schools in respect to the new pupil intake and also carried out further screening and diagnostic tests on such pupils. They also took up referrals from subject teachers, made both during pupils' first year of secondary schooling and consequently. Where collaborative work with subject teachers took place, it seemed that information was both requested and disseminated more widely than previously, when the remedial department had been more isolated, since collaborative work offered more opportunities to discuss pupils with teachers (cf.Clunies-Ross and Wimhurst,1983). Moreover, where the remedial department was more integrated with other departments, subject teachers did seem to consider that the information gathered by remedial teachers from screening and diagnosis was a 'whole school' resource rather than a resource for the remedial department alone to carry out its work. It could well be the case therefore that the implementation of redefined remedial education will enhance the importance of the traditional assessment role.

In respect to responsibility for specialised remedial tuition and counselling, the picture may be more complex. The development of collaborative work between remedial and subject teacher could be seen as a way of further integrating pupils with learning difficulties in the mainstream classroom, since with appropriate methods and materials, such pupils may be able to 'cope' with mainstream work and indeed even develop their learning skills. However not all subject teachers will necessarily accept all responsibility for all learning problems and they may well continue to consider that some withdrawal for specialised help from a remedial teacher is appropriate. Two Scottish studies (Clark et al,1982, Ferguson and Adams,1982) found a considerable amount of support for some withdrawal of pupils for specialised remedial tuition, from the subject teachers interviewed, and in my own research, as suggested in the last chapter, although teachers considered that the integration of pupils with learning difficulties in the mainstream class had a number of social and academic benefits, many also believed that small withdrawal groups and specialised remedial tuition should be maintained, particularly for pupils with severe literacy problems. Such groups were seen to provide the individual attention needed for such problems and the specialist expertise in severe literacy difficulties held by remedial teachers, an expertise which subject teachers felt they did not possess.

Thus the development of 'remedial education across the curriculum' may not necessarily remove a perceived need for specialised remedial tuition in basic literacy and numeracy. Support and advice from the remedial teacher may extend the parameters of what is considered to be an acceptable prerequisite level of literacy, in that subject teachers may be more able to adapt materials and teaching methods with the help of the remedial teacher. However, responsibility for teaching pupils with the more severe difficulties, to improve their basic skills, may still remain with the subject teacher.

There is no reason why such traditional responsibilities should not be fulfilled in conjunction with a cross-curricular role. However if no additional remedial staffing is provided, then such responsibility is likely to impinge on the opportunities and time available to develop work with subject departments. A number of the remedial teachers whom I interviewed commented on the difficulties of establishing priorities for remedial staffing allocation, noting in particular that time to work with other departments was severely curtailed by the time given to specialised individual or group tuition. As one remedial teacher explained,

> it is very frustrating. You are given a blank timetable, you have to decide priorities and then justify those priorities and at the same time explain to the Head or whoever why we have not dealt with Fred Bloggs and his reading. On the one hand I am working with, say, a group of two kids and am trying to do a good thing with them and yet they are costing me six periods a week which I could be spending with a class and

hopefully getting a wider change.

Despite, therefore, intentions to develop more work across the curriculum, such work may be constrained by traditional responsibilities. Nor will it necessarily be possible or even desirable to reduce such commitments to responsibilities like basic literacy tuition. Subject teachers may feel they do not have the necessary expertise to help some pupils, so that the remedial teacher has to give them some tuition and remedial teachers too, may consider such work to be an important part of their overall role.

Traditional responsibilities and expertise are therefore unlikely to be abandoned after the implementation of redefined remedial education. At the same time some new expertise would seem to be needed. The traditional expertise of remedial teachers has resided in their capacity to make individual diagnoses of learning difficulties and draw on appropriate knowledge and skills to remediate the identified problems. In many ways it can perhaps be suggested that cross-curricular work is just an extension of such expertise into a different context, namely subject teaching and mainstream teaching groups. However the provision of advice and help on materials and teaching methods in such a new context would seem to require some knowledge of subjects, of curriculum development and of methods of organisation and teaching for large teaching groups. In addition, the interaction between remedial and subject teacher presumed in the 'new partnership' would seem to require new interpersonal skills.

Certainly the remedial teachers whom I interviewed were very aware of the need for a different expertise. Like the subject teachers whom I interviewed, they did not necessarily feel that lack of knowledge of a subject would preclude remedial teachers from working with subject teachers. Knowledge of a particular subject could gradually be built up, through discussion, reading and preparation for support work. Like many of the subject teachers interviewed, they also considered that the work normally undertaken by pupils with learning difficulties was at a level which could be reasonably easily understood. Nevertheless knowledge of a subject did afford confidence and facilitated the giving of better advice and help. Sometimes lack of knowledge could also be a barrier to collaborative work, especially, it was felt, in

the fourth and fifth year of secondary schooling,
where the subject became more complex. Thus these
remedial teachers wanted in-service training to help
them carry out their new role, a training which
would give them more knowledge about individual
subjects, about classroom management and teaching
methods, about curriculum development and about some
of the wider educational issues now confronting
secondary schools. Many also commented that they
sometimes found advisory and support work difficult
to carry out in terms of how to give advice
effectively and so on, which suggests that training
on these aspects of the new role might also be
useful.

The redefinition of remedial education thus
presumes some changes in the traditional expertise
of remedial teachers. However it does not seem that
this new expertise is necessarily incompatible with
traditional knowledge and methods. Nevertheless
changes in the expertise and knowledge of a subject
community can present difficulties for some members.
It may result in the 'de-skilling' of segments of
the community, particularly those whose professional
training and experience has been based on a previous
definition of practice. Thus career structures and
opportunities may be altered. For example, when
looking at the redefinition of school mathematics,
Cooper found that older non-graduate teachers were
partially deskilled and materials and approaches
were introduced which their educational perspectives
could not easily accommodate. Younger teachers
promoting 'modern maths' represented a threat to
their sense of seniority during re-organisation
(1983,p.218). It may well be that the redefinition
of remedial education will similarly threaten those
remedial teachers whose skills reside primarily in
the provision of literacy and numeracy coaching for
groups of pupils extracted from the mainstream or
who do not wish to work across the curriculum. As
one remedial teacher commented to me:

> I can still see a lot of people in remedial
> work have not got the requisite qualities to
> work from department to department, they are
> not well educated, they have not got the
> confidence, because their world has just been
> sat in a little room with a little group of
> kids. And how can they walk out and be the
> big, executive, senior management and say 'This
> is what I want, this is what we are going to
> do, we are going to integrate across all these

areas and this is how we are going to do it'. They simply have not got the expertise to do it.

Such required changes in remedial expertise are likely to be dependent on in-service training rather than the content and approach of initial studies and training received[1]. Unlike change in some subjects therefore, age and initial training will not necessarily preclude the adoption of a new expertise. Nevertheless, older remedial teachers may find it difficult to accommodate to a redefinition, because such change will involve a radical alteration of previous perceptions and practice. They also may simply not possess the 'career structure' appropriate to the redefined role, no matter how much they be willing to change. Indeed it could be suggested that remedial teachers of whatever age who have only specialised in traditional remedial education will not have the appropriate expertise and career structure which will facilitate obtaining the more senior posts. When I questioned management staff about the type of qualities and experience which might now be considered appropriate for a head of a remedial department operating a policy of 'remedial education across the curriculum', many considered that they would look for traditional expertise in the area of learning difficulties but also stressed the value of perhaps having been a subject teacher, having some experience of curriculum development and in particular, the importance of having the personal qualities needed to work closely with other teachers, as a consequence of experience of previous team work. These qualities were also mentioned by the remedial teachers interviewed as being requisite to the new role. Some remedial teachers may therefore find that their expertise and experience may no longer facilitate movement up the career structure.

Thus the redefinition of remedial education may not necessarily result in increased status for all remedial teachers. For some it may involve the 'spoiling' of career and the negation of status and expertise. In addition redefinition may have other consequences for professional fulfilment. For example, the remedial teachers whom I interviewed felt that the 'new role' could be quite stressful. It could be very tiring and difficult to obtain more expertise in different subjects, as one remedial teacher explained:

It is very draining. You have to look at the background materials, what is good science teaching, what it is about. Or French. I found myself reading more and more, what was deemed to be good practice by the editors of books and so on. If you are in a classroom, I like to think I know a little bit about what is good in science or geography, what is expected of the good teacher in that subject area. So there is that as well as trying to do the daily work. Very exciting but very tiring.

In addition, the work of being in a number of departments could give rise to stress, since the remedial teacher had to switch continuously from one subject to another. And working with individual teachers could be stressful simply because of the need to adapt to every individual teacher's 'style' or methods, even where the individuals taught the same subject. Working across the curriculum, remedial teachers could lose their 'identity', or the security of expected routine or the fulfilment of seeing the outcome of personal involvement over time with a group or class. Then too, success with cross-curricular work was dependent on the actions of other teachers and where they did not wish to change, the remedial teacher remained powerless. As one remedial teacher commented,

> the thing I find most stressful is when you find something you disagree with but you can't do anything about it, that is awful. You may be supportive, doing work in a department but they have organised themselves in a way you don't agree with. And then some of the work you are putting in, it's just going down the drain, you are supporting a system which will not work.

Also, despite an apparent involvement across the curriculum and the development of policies which had integrated remedial provision, the remedial teacher could still feel marginal and ineffective, particularly where resources and time to establish change (and continuity) were limited:

> You are in a position where you are neither coming nor going, you are a satellite orbiting the school. Where possible, you have to sneak in, do your bit, sneak out, sneak in again.

You can look at the number of departments, the amount of influence you have got, the pure logistics means that perhaps you could work with Science and Maths one year and that is perhaps with only one year of a course. And then Humanities the next year, perhaps only with courses in the first two years ... You might get some success and then you have got to go off to another department and start from square one again and then by that time the other department may have had a few changes of staff ...

Nevertheless, despite these difficulties, it was generally considered that working across the curriculum, giving support and help to pupils and to teachers, had a number of advantages. As one teacher commented, despite the stresses of working in a number of different lessons and continuously having to come up with helpful ideas,

you must take the other side of the coin. If I go into an English lesson and it is brilliant, or another lesson and something is good, you can pass those things on. There are benefits.

By being involved in a variety of lessons and departments, the remedial teacher could disseminate good ideas and methods from one teacher to another and could also act as a central focus for the development of policies and practice within the school. It was also considered that by working alongside subject teachers in the mainstream curriculum, remedial teachers could be more effective. From such work and discussion it was possible to develop

a greater understanding between us and departments, of the kids who are failing, or, which is important, of the methods which are failing. And if you do that you have a much better chance of avoiding problems than you do if you are not having that type of consultation. It is easy then to pick up things which are going wrong, and rectify. And that means you are tackling the problem at the very source rather than waiting for the children to fail. You can identify problems before they become so.

It was also considered that such an approach avoided

131

the 'labelling' or 'stigma' which could be experienced by pupils with learning difficulties when they were in special classes or withdrawn for long periods for extra remedial help and this integration of pupils in mainstream classes also gave such pupils access to the specialist knowledge of subject teachers, a knowledge which could not be provided by remedial teachers alone taking such pupils for help and for lessons. Some did suggest that pupils could then miss some of the benefits of a small group, such as security, close relationships and individual help with basic difficulties, but it was generally considered that working across the curriculum had a number of advantages in terms of improving provision for pupils with learning difficulties. In any case, work with small groups was not seen to be incompatible with such a cross-curricular role, and additional remedial help, on an individual basis or in small groups was provided for those pupils considered to need it.

The redefinition of remedial education thus seems to offer a number of advantages and disadvantages from the remedial teacher's point of view. It offers the satisfaction of developing an approach to provision which seems to be less stigmatising for pupils and more effective in that problems may be tackled at their source. Collaborative work, as some remedial teachers also commented, can also be more stimulating and challenging than just being responsible for small groups of pupils needing help with basic skills. At the same time there can be the frustrations of not having enough staffing and time to develop such work, or where it has been implemented, of not necessarily being able to change things as desired. It can also be tiring and stressful working with a number of teachers and subjects and would seem to require changes in expertise which take time and energy to develop, and for some teachers, such changes and the new requirements of the remedial teacher's role may 'spoil' their careers[2].

Finally, in respect to the prospects for instituting change, several issues seem to be important. Firstly, remedial teachers do not always have the power or status to implement change. Any 'partnership' between remedial and subject teacher will involve some negotiation, a point that was discussed in the last chapter. This aspect of 'partnership' was also recognised by the remedial teachers I interviewed, and whilst it was accepted, they often felt management support was needed, to sustain their status and 'bargaining power'. However even with such support, given the legacies of traditional low status, the continuing dominance of subject hierarchies and the pervasive influence of subject sub-culture and other professional norms such as the importance of autonomy, those negotiations may be difficult to realise in terms which reflect the ideas and practices of remedial teachers. Secondly, whatever the problems of 'partnership', the constraints of not having enough remedial staffing and time to develop collaborative work may inhibit its implementation. In addition, although traditional expertise and practice may seem to be compatible with new approaches, traditional responsibilities for special tuition may well further impinge on the limited resources already available for work across the curriculum. Some remedial teachers may also not be willing to implement a redefined remedial education, because it conflicts with their definitions of 'good practice', because of lack of expertise, because of the stresses and difficulties it may bring or because of the implications it may have for their careers, and this may further inhibit change. If the redefinition of remedial education is to be successfully implemented in schools, these issues will have to be given a lot more consideration. Some further aspects of redefinition, as they affect pupils, will now be discussed.

REDEFINITION AND PUPILS WITH LEARNING DIFFICULTIES

There has been very little research on the views of pupils with learning difficulties about the kind of remedial help they would prefer. Research on pupils within remedial education has concentrated on the identification and causes of their learning difficulties and on methods and materials which could be used to teach them. Although it might be recognised that 'motivation' or past experience of failure are important to pupil progress, the perspectives of pupils in relation to their learning difficulties have been less widely discussed and there has been little consideration as to whether those difficulties are best dealt with in small groups, through withdrawal or through mainstream help, from the pupil's point of view.

Yet the perspectives and actions of pupils are of major importance in relation to the way the curriculum and organisation of the school are realised. As Hammersley and Woods have commented,

> There can be little doubt that pupils' own interpretations of school processes represent a crucial link in the educational chain. Unless we understand how pupils respond to different forms of pedagogy and school organisation and why they respond in the ways they do, our efforts to increase the effectiveness or to change the impact of schooling will stand little chance of success.
> (1984,p.3)

Pupils may have very different perspectives from teachers. Classroom interaction, between teacher and pupil, involves a negotiation of 'definitions of the situation' in respect to both teacher's control of pupils and the organisation of learning. Pupils may test out teachers' reactions to different types of behaviour, to find out what sorts of behaviour and what levels of work effort will be tolerated and what may lead to castigation or punishment. Pupils may also seek to resist or renegotiate teachers' definitions of learning situations or subjects[3]. The pupils' perspective may thus be important when looking at approaches to learning difficulties particularly where the interest or difficulties of subjects are being considered or new ways of teaching are being tried. Unfortunately there seems to be very little research on the views of pupils with learning difficulties on particular subjects and the methods by which they are taught[4].

There is also the issue of pupil grouping and how it may affect pupils with learning difficulties. Studies of the differentiation of pupils within the secondary school have shown how pupils in lower ability groups come to evaluate themselves in terms of their organisational status and a process of polarisation may then take place within the pupil population, whereby pupils group themselves round either pro- or anti-school norms, with anti-school norms being more prevalent in lower ability groups[5]. When looking therefore at pupils' perceived problems, especially in regard to issues like the 'motivation' of pupils with learning difficulties, it is important to look at the context of that 'motivation' and consider whether perhaps pupils are not so much lacking in motivation as responding to the way in which they have been defined. The issue of teacher expectations also needs to be considered. Pupils may well respond to certain expectations of performance and such expectations may also influence interactions between teachers and pupils[6]. Certainly where only academic success is valued, pupils with learning difficulties may well feel rejected and consider themselves to be 'failures' and not work effectively in consequence. For as Sewell has noted, such constant rejection communicates itself and low attainers are thus more likely to become bored, withdrawn or disruptive (1982,p.8). They may be less likely to take intellectual risks and if asked for an answer in a lesson, may fall back on a repertoire of techniques to escape investigation (Holt,1969).

Holt has also highlighted the differences in perception between pupils and teachers in respect to the central aims of school. He suggested that

> for children the central business of school ... is getting these daily tasks done, or at least out of the way, with a minimum of effort and unpleasantness. Each task is an end in itself. The children don't care how they dispose of it. If they can get it out of the way by doing it, they will do it; if experience has taught them that this does not work very well, they will turn to other means, illegitimate means, that wholly defeat whatever purpose the task-giver may have had in mind.
> (ibid.,p.37)

Such discrepancies between the teacher's view and the pupil's view were also suggested by some of the teachers whom I interviewed during my research. For example, commenting on some of the problems presented by pupils with learning difficulties in lessons, an English teacher considered that

> a lot of work seems to be done for extraneous reasons, they come to school because they are expected to. In some cases it is more positive but the actual gleaning of knowledge, understanding things, acquiring experience and all that lot doesn't seem to feature as important ... (then there is) this nice tidy idea of what is right and wrong, we are here to do what the teachers want, not for anything else, so if there is a question, for example, 'What did the boy do in the story', their question is 'What is correct?' and never mind motives beyond that ... the whole purpose is different. The teacher may be thinking the

purpose is one thing, the kids will be doing just one tiny aspect of that purpose. But I am sure that is true of other lessons too - in history, for example, (they are told) 'Don't just say what caused whatever it is, say the second world war, but explain, expound, add' and they will tend not to, to say 'Why (should I), we have got an answer there.'

Thus pupils with learning difficulties may have a very instrumental attitude to school work - get things done as quickly and easily as possible and out of the way. Such an attitude is perhaps not surprising given that school work may be difficult and constantly invoke feelings of failure. When looking at issues like 'motivation' or even ability to produce good work, it is thus important to recognise the pupil's perspective and consider that 'failure' may not be so much a consequence of lack of ability or motivation as the result of a perspective which dismisses work as a necessary but uninviting and unimportant chore.

At the same time, it is important to recognise that such instrumentalism or perceptions of school work as irrelevant, may be only part of the picture. Furlong (1977), for instance, studying a group of 'below average' girls in a secondary modern school found that how much they could learn in class was extremely important to them. They seemed to enjoy the sense of achievement which came from filling up exercise books with notes, or typing something correctly or getting good marks in a test. They preferred rigidly structured work, with a concrete product, such as notes, and where they felt the teacher provided opportunities for working and learning, they responded positively. Otherwise, they were disruptive. Evans (1985) has also suggested that difficult behaviour may arise not so much because of negative pupil attitudes but because of frustration at not being able to learn properly. Where work is too difficult, or sufficient teacher time and attention are not available, and teachers do not therefore, create conditions for successful learning, dissatisfaction with content and instruction may emerge. (pp.153-55). The solution to disaffection from pupils with learning difficulties may not lie therefore in a change in pupil attitude but in a change in teaching methods (a point that would no doubt be made by many remedial teachers and which also can be used to support the development of cross-curricular remedial work).

The issues raised by a consideration of pupils' perspectives are thus quite complex. There is a need for far more research on these issues as they pertain to pupils with learning difficulties, in order to understand how learning experiences and learning problems affect and are interpreted by such pupils. A greater sensitivity to the views of pupils could make remedial provision and subject teaching more effective. It might also help to resolve some of the problems raised by the organisation of remedial provision and facilitate a greater awareness of some of the possible implications of redefinition for the pupils concerned. These questions will now be briefly discussed.

A major problem, when considering the organisation of remedial provision, concerns the relative advantages and disadvantages of extraction or withdrawal, special classes or providing remedial help in the mainstream class. Integration, rather than withdrawal or a special class, can be seen to have both academic and social advantages. A study by Capron et al (1983) found that as segregated remedial pupils progressed through the school, they tended to adopt increasingly 'antisocial' behaviours and hostile attitudes to their more able peers, to indicate a preference to be taught separately and to achieve a low standard of academic work. Integration, on the other hand, improved behaviour and attitudes, increased the desire for integration and improved the standard of work. Herndon (1972) also suggests that special classes may have a negative effect on pupils. His pupils considered themselves to be the 'dumb class' and he could not overcome their lack of intellectual confidence. The skills they exercised in shops or the bowling alley simply could not be transferred to school. When confronted by questions about shopping or scoring in class, they came up with all the wrong answers and no longer trusted their ability to give the right answers, even though out of class they managed extremely well. Even where withdrawal is used rather than a special class, pupils may not respond well. Gordon cites the case of one pupil he encountered who did not want help with his spelling because he would be highlighted as different and inferior if taken out from class. Gordon suggests that

the act of withdrawal from the ordinary class

even for a short assessment is often a shaming experience for young people.
(1983,p.176)

At the same time, being given extra help in class may also 'show up' those pupils who receive it and they may feel embarrassed by the presence of the remedial teacher. One of the remedial teachers whom I interviewed made this very point:

The arguments (for support in class) are that he won't get singled out as a remedial child, that he is learning the same things as other pupils, because obviously when they come to you, they can't learn the same things, you don't know, say, what the geography teacher is doing, you haven't got the work. But the three I go in to, they feel very embarrassed the moment I walk through the door. And they look at each other and they know they need my help but they hate it. The other kids see it. At least before they could come to my room and then no-one could see inside. Now that doesn't exist.

Of course it may be possible to avoid 'showing up' such pupils by sharing the help given by the remedial teacher amongst all the pupils in the class or by organising support so that the remedial teacher may take the 'whole class' and the subject teacher spends time with those needing help. Then such pupils may not be so closely identified with the remedial teacher. However some subject teachers may still prefer the remedial teacher to concentrate on those pupils who have difficulties and it could be argued that the remedial teacher's expertise should focus on pupils seen to most need it. When I gave support to pupils in mainstream classes, I found responses were mixed. Some pupils did not like it, for fear of being 'shown up' but others quite frequently requested some help with problems. Interestingly enough, when such work first started, it was the 'non-target' pupils who seemed to most frequently question the team teaching/support role of a remedial teacher and the legitimacy of the remedial teacher's involvement in subject lessons. Investigation of pupils' perspectives on remedial work should perhaps not only be limited to pupils with learning difficulties. The views and responses of other pupils formerly rarely having contact with a remedial teacher may be an important consideration in respect to the development of any new role for remedial teachers.

In addition to considering the sensitive deployment of team teaching support within the mainstream classroom, it might be useful to examine further the views of pupils in respect to which form of provision they would find most helpful and least stigmatising. In discussions with some of my former pupils, I found a range of views on these issues. The older pupils, who had been in a 'remedial class', before the system was changed to withdrawal and support in class, were very aware of the problems which could be encountered in giving them extra help. The majority favoured integration, since then they would be learning the same things as their peers and other pupils could then not make fun of them. They also felt that being in a remedial class could deny certain chances or opportunities, in terms of option choice in the fourth year or at least 'having a go' at the ordinary curriculum. As one boy said,

> If I had gone in the next class up, I could have adapted, even though I am not brainy.

On the other hand, some felt that being in a small, special class 'gave you a chance to get more help' and you could get 'shown up' in the ordinary class since 'you might not be so good at reading aloud' or might not be able to do the work. The younger pupils, who were withdrawn or supported in class, also had mixed feelings. Some did not want to come to withdrawal groups, fearing that other pupils would 'make fun of them'. Others said they liked the extra attention of a small group and the opportunity to improve their skills or indeed, 'escape' from lessons which they found particularly difficult.

It may not be easy therefore to draw any general conclusions about the views of pupils. However, at least their views could be taken into account. Gordon (op.cit.) has pointed out that the concept of partnership with parents incorporated into the 1981 Education Act should also be extended where possible to older children and young persons. They should thus be involved in decision making about receiving extra help. Certainly to explain the arguments for special tuition and to allow pupils to weigh the advantages and disadvantages would acknowledge that pupils themselves are sensitive to the issues, and their perspectives are an important facet of any remediation of learning difficulties. Equally, perhaps parents should be involved in discussing decisions, for pupils of any age, so that they are aware of the issues and can provide support at home. Recent studies have demonstrated that parental involvement can play a significant part in the improvement of reading[7]. The 1981 Education Act also allows for parental involvement. If pupils' and their parents' views were taken into account, remedial help, however it is provided, could be far more effective.

These are some of the ways, therefore, in which the pupil's perspective could be acknowledged. Equally, when looking at other aspects of remedial education, such as assessment, the pupil's view should be taken into account. Pupils may well have considerable awareness of their difficulties and of what may be causing certain problems. If the pupil's views and explanations can be examined, this may help with both the choice and the effectiveness of remedial teaching. Moreover, if more understanding and knowledge of pupils' interpretations and definitions of situations can be developed, this may provide useful insights into the processes of teaching and learning in both remedial groups and mainstream classes. The implications of redefining remedial education in respect to the situation and experiences of the pupils concerned might then be more fully understood, providing a more substantive basis for decisions on strategies, teaching approaches and the organisation of provision.

Nevertheless, whatever the attention paid to the perspectives of pupils, the degree to which radical change can be wrought in their learning experiences and in their position in school, will have to be seriously considered. High status, academic knowledge remains dominant within schools, together with a definition of achievement which stresses attainments in cognitive skills and knowledge. Until such definitions and status are changed, those who have some difficulty with such knowledge and skills are likely to continue to be regarded as 'less able', 'slow' or 'failures'. Thus although the redefinition of remedial education may facilitate some changes in the integration and curricular experiences of pupils with learning difficulties, it may not substantially change the way in which such pupils are viewed, and their subsequent low and marginal status is likely to remain a feature of their school experience.

Moreover it cannot be assumed that learning experiences will indeed be significantly improved with the development of 'remedial education across the curriculum'. It was argued in Chapter Three that many of the teaching approaches and methods which may be instituted for pupils with learning difficulties may be no more than 'coping strategies'. Given the current material conditions of teaching, however conscientious the intention, it may not be possible to teach to 'individual need' and indeed such an approach may lead to further differentiation of pupils with learning difficulties. Certainly if the redefinition of remedial education is to be regarded as being more effective than traditional measures, some attention will have to be paid to its evaluation in terms of the learning outcomes and experiences of pupils. Such evaluation may be particularly problematic, given the many 'variables' of pupil difficulties, 'partnerships' between remedial and subject teacher, modes of teaching, resources and school context, and the diversity of practices within subjects and remedial teaching, but it will be very important if arguments for redefinition are to be sustained and beneficial consequences realised. Then perhaps with such empirical findings and a consideration of the issues and problems involved, some amelioration of pupils' experiences and learning problems may be achieved. However, if the situation of pupils with learning difficulties is to alter within schools, wide curricular and organisational change will have to be very much the focus of activity and policies and practices directed towards these ends be carefully thought out. Some of these policies and practices will now be considered.

NOTES

1. The majority of remedial teachers are trained/work in other subjects before becoming remedial teachers. Such initial training may therefore be less important in terms of remedial teachers' careers and willingness/ability to adopt change.
2. The question of the 'interests' of remedial teachers thus needs careful examination. Although redefinition may serve certain material interests it may also threaten 'survival' through increased stress or demands on limited expertise. Material benefits and the satisfaction of implementing perceived 'good practice' may thus conflict with

other 'survival interests'. The degree to which redefinition serves all the interests of remedial teachers (and of all remedial teachers, given the potential 'spoiling' of some careers) needs to be questioned. Similarly, if it is going to be suggested that special education serves the 'interests' of its professionals (e.g. Tomlinson,1982) then more consideration needs to be given to the various dimensions of those 'interests' and to some of the contradictions which may be involved. Morever, if certain remedial teachers do not agree with redefinition or may experience a 'spoiling' of career, whose interests are then being served by redefinition? As suggested in Chapter Two, the reasons for the promulgation and acceptance of new approaches need closer investigation, together with some consideration of the implications which redefinition may have for the 'communal identity' of all remedial teachers.

3.   For example, Milner (1978) found that his pupils did not enjoy 'new geography', were put off by its scientific and mathematical approach and considered it was not 'real geography' preferring the study of exotic foreign places. Spradbery (1976) found that the innovatory material of 'Mathematics for the Majority' was resisted by the very pupils for whom it was designed, being considered to be too 'babyish', not 'proper maths' and an obstacle to progress as the pupils defined it.

4.   Wilson (1982c) however has carried out some research on attitudes to history, which suggests that its relevance is questioned, it is considered to be difficult and teaching and learning methods are a source of dissatisfaction. It would seem therefore that the congruence of pupils' and teachers' views cannot be assumed and that more consideration needs to be given to the views of pupils with learning difficulties.

5.   Such research was of course not primarily concerned with pupils with learning difficulties and remedial forms were not investigated in studies like those of Hargreaves (1967) or Ball (1981). The evidence available on remedial classes is also somewhat contradictory. Ball (ibid.) notes that they were regarded as being more docile than middle band forms by the teachers at Beachside and King (1983) notes a similar paradox. However, as will shortly be discussed, other studies suggest that segregation in a remedial class can lead to unfavourable school attitudes. Some further

research would thus be useful and could also consider the more elaborate models of pupil adaptation now being put forward (see Woods,1983,pp.89-96).

6. The issue of teacher expectations and pupil performance is complex. However Brophy and Good (1974) for example, have suggested that teacher expectations can affect such performance and self-esteem and that teachers also interact more positively with high expectation pupils, giving them more praise and less criticism than low expectation pupils. This aspect of pupil-teacher relationships does need careful consideration and more research on teacher expectations of, and interaction with, pupils with learning difficulties would be extremely useful.

7. e.g. Hewison (1982).

Chapter Six

THE DEVELOPMENT OF POLICIES AND PRACTICE

A NEW THEORETICAL FRAMEWORK

It has been suggested during this analysis of the
redefinition of remedial education that the new role
posited for the remedial teacher will demand a new
expertise. The development of an expertise
appropriate to cross-curricular work will require
changes in the theoretical framework of remedial
education. As Sewell has commented in his book on
the reshaping of remedial education, in constructing
such a theoretical framework it has been usual to
conceive of the child and his needs as the focus and
the school and its social context as peripheral
(1982,p.5). Thus traditionally, remedial education
has been dominated by what might be termed the
'psychological paradigm'. Research and practice
have been primarily devoted to discovering the
causes of learning difficulties and handicaps, to
improving assessment procedures and to developing
materials and techniques for remediation. However
the redefinition of remedial education would seem to
require an extension of this theoretical framework
and knowledge, to take account of the new
involvement with the mainstream curriculum and with
the social processes and context of the mainstream
school. To facilitate the implementation of the
redefinition of remedial education, remedial
teachers will need to draw on sociological and
curriculum theory, knowledge and research.
     This is not to suggest that the psychological
approach to learning difficulties should be
abandoned. Remedial teachers will continue to need
to use psychological knowledge about learning
difficulties in order to develop appropriate
assessment, teaching techniques and materials. It
is also not being suggested that sociological and

144

curriculum theory has been previously ignored. Ways of looking at teaching methods, curriculum design and materials within remedial education have been usefully drawn from the curriculum literature[1]. Recognition has also been given to the interaction of social and individual factors in learning difficulties[2]. However, sociological and curriculum knowledge and research need to occupy a more central position within the theoretical framework of remedial education if the implementation of redefinition is to be successful. How then could this theoretical framework be developed and what would such development entail?

The field of curriculum study offers a considerable potential for the development of new expertise and for the development of greater understanding about the processes and implications of redefinition. As already noted, current practice in remedial teaching does draw on models of curriculum design and on new ideas about teaching methods. Many of these may well be appropriate to cross-curricular work and this possibility should be more fully investigated. Cross-curricular work will also require more knowledge about the content and pedagogy of individual subjects and about methods and materials appropriate for the teaching of pupils with learning difficulties. The literature on such questions is beginning to develop[3] and further contributions by both subject specialists and remedial teachers need to be encouraged. Equally, the organisation of teaching and teaching groups within mainstream classes needs to be more fully considered, in order to develop successful strategies for the teaching of pupils with learning difficulties[4]. In addition, if 'whole school policies' towards remedial provision are to be developed, remedial teachers will need to know more about the wider implications and principles of curriculum planning, so that such provision becomes an integral part of the whole school curriculum.

Given that the redefinition of remedial education is a form of curriculum innovation, one of the most valuable aspects of curriculum research and study might be that which is concerned with such innovation. Indeed McNicholas has already argued that remedial teachers' deliberations could gain significantly from a study of the literature on curriculum change (1979,p.151). It has been argued in previous chapters that remedial teachers should consider the experience of other innovations, in particular the consistent experience that the outcome of innovation has differed from the original intentions of the innovators. Such experience has led to more consideration of the importance of the innovating context and the effect which it may have on proposed change. In particular, the influence and importance of teachers' beliefs and practices has been accorded greater scrutiny. A wider knowledge of curriculum innovation, as part of the theoretical framework of remedial teaching, could thus perhaps facilitate better approaches to innovation in remedial education, the success of which is likely to greatly depend on teachers' beliefs and practices and changes in the curriculum and organisation within particular school contexts. Such knowledge could also help to develop strategies for innovation. Bennis, Benn and Chin (1961) for example, offer a typology of strategies, namely the 'rational-empirical', 'normative-reeducative' and 'power-coercive' approaches to change, which could be used to analyse innovation in remedial education[5] and writers such as Hoyle (1971) have discussed the role of the 'change agent', discussion which could be used to help develop the role of the remedial teacher.

Equally, sociological analysis and research could usefully become a part of the theoretical framework of remedial education. Many of the issues which have been discussed in previous chapters, such as subject sub-culture, school curricula, pedagogical practice, pupil perspectives and strategies and the selective functions of schools have been the focus of considerable sociological research[6] which could be used to develop analysis of remedial education and its role within schools. In addition, sociological approaches to special education are beginning to be developed[7] and such sociological perspectives could be used to think more critically about the tenets and practices of remedial education and about the consequences of new policies and change. Given that the redefinition of remedial education does posit a new engagement with mainstream education and the construction of a new interface between 'special' and 'ordinary' teaching, a more critical and wider understanding of the issues and processes which may be involved would seem to be crucial. Such understanding could well be developed by the use of the 'sociological imagination' within the theoretical framework of remedial education. It would also aid the development of appropriate policies and practice, some of which will now be discussed.

'PARTNERSHIPS' AND 'WHOLE SCHOOL POLICIES'

The 'new partnership' with subject teachers has been posited as one means of developing 'remedial education across the curriculum'. It has also been suggested that such development could be further facilitated by 'whole school policies' on remedial provision. Yet, as was noted in Chapter Two, very little attention has been paid to the precise meaning of such partnerships and policies or to the ways in which they could be implemented, despite their importance as means of change.

The notion of 'partnership' does seem to imply an equal and collaborative relationship between the remedial and subject teacher. However such relationships are not always easy to establish in practice. As was discussed in Chapter Four, a study by Ferguson and Adams (1982) found remedial teachers were often relegated to the position of 'teacher's aide' rather than equal 'partner'. It was also suggested in the same chapter that conflicts could arise over teaching methods and content and that such 'partnerships' could be subject to considerable negotiation. Not all experiences of collaboration may involve conflict of course, and it may be fairly easily resolved. Bowie and Robertson, for example, found that although cooperative teaching between mathematics and remedial teachers started from a conflict of perspectives, eventually 'our erstwhile differing views began to fuse' (1985,p.129). Nevertheless, given the issue of professional autonomy and the possible differences in respect to curriculum content and pedagogy which are to be found amongst subject and remedial teachers, it has to be acknowledged that the concept of 'partnership' can be problematic.

It was suggested in Chapter Four that by unpacking the beliefs and processes involved in the construction of such a 'partnership' and by paying particular attention to issues like autonomy, to subject sub-culture and to other professional norms and definitions of 'good practice', the remedial teacher, and indeed, the subject teacher, may begin to identify what constitutes any problems of 'partnership'. Some resolution of such problems, perhaps a negotiated 'compromise' may then be reached. At the same time, 'negotiation' and 'compromise' may bring their own difficulties. If remedial teachers do indeed have (or believe they

147

have) some appropriate answers and some better approaches to the teaching of pupils with learning difficulties and these are not fully accepted, then there may be a sense of frustration, and if indeed these approaches are better, improved provision and teaching will not be achieved. Further discussion may of course result in the desired change, but it cannot be assumed that this will occur. Certainly, the implications of having to work in a 'negotiated' or 'compromise' situation, which at best may indeed be a partnership but at worst could be no more than an uneasy 'truce' do need to be considered.

It could be argued that many 'partnerships' have been successfully implemented and that to focus on potential problems is to deny the many advantages and possibilities of collaboration. Nevertheless, given the strength of subject sub-cultures and of the issue of autonomy within the occupational culture of teachers, it is likely that many remedial teachers will have some difficulty in establishing such collaborative work. Team teaching and other forms of joint work between teachers even of the same subject can be difficult enough to establish. The remedial teacher has to work with teachers of different subjects and also overcome past or current low and marginal status. Even if remedial teachers do not want the power and status to impose their 'definition of the situation' on other teachers, they will need enough power and status to ensure an 'equal say'. Both past legacies and current structure and perceptions may seriously impinge on both that power and that status.

Nevertheless such 'partnerships' may well be successfully established. Where this is the case, it could be useful to look carefully at the factors which may have contributed to that success. How, for example, was such collaboration initiated - at the request of the subject or the remedial teacher and did that seem to have a bearing on its development? What issues needed to be discussed and how were any conflicts resolved? Did the collaboration primarily focus on content and materials or on teaching methods and did that particular focus make it easier to work together? If team teaching took place, how was it organised, and was it aided by a particular form of teaching organisation, such as individual, resource-based learning or group work? Might it have been less successful in a different organisational context? And was it aided by a particular 'climate' within the school, for example, by teachers' general agreement that collaboration and team work was 'good practice'? If remedial and subject teachers were to consider the elements of successful collaboration, and disseminate their experiences accordingly, it might be possible to more clearly understand the processes and contexts through and in which the 'spirit of compromise' begins to operate and 'erstwhile differing views' begin to 'fuse' (Bowie and Robertson, op.cit.).

Such understanding may thus help to elaborate and refine the concept of 'partnership'. In addition though, if 'partnership' is to be seen as a major means of realising a redefinition of remedial education, it may be inappropriate to characterise remedial teachers as 'change agents', as sharers of their expertise. Such a model of change is somewhat one-sided in that it tends to give primacy to the expertise of remedial teachers, and to their rationales for and interpretations of change. It thus implicitly reduces the importance of the views and interpretations of other participants and highlights issues of professional autonomy. A participatory model, in which rationales are jointly explored and expertise jointly modified might offer a better framework for 'partnership'. Exchange of experience might also be used to develop a greater mutual understandng of respective responsibilities and interests. If the remedial teacher was a class teacher for some time during the week, this would afford more than theoretical recognition of the pressures and constraints on subject teachers. Equally, subject teachers taking a small group or working alongside another subject teacher, giving support to pupils with learning difficulties, might more fully understand some of the difficulties of the remedial teacher's teaching and cross-curricular roles. Potential conflicts of approach and the issues of status and power would not be solved in such ways, but they might facilitate a greater understanding of what collaborative working can involve. Certainly, if the 'partnership' with subject teachers is going to be one of the major means of implementing 'remedial education across the curriculum', it would seem to need a lot more detailed and careful consideration.

Equally there needs to be more consideration of the development of 'whole school policies'. As noted in Chapter Two, although the importance of such policies is often mooted, the precise ways in which they may be developed and agreed have been given less attention. The problems of reconciling a diversity of views and practices within a school have not been widely examined and nor is it entirely clear what exactly a 'whole school policy' should be. Should it be primarily a statement of aims and objectives or should it be concerned with more detailed prescription about the role of the remedial teacher and methods of providing for pupils with learning difficulties across the curriculum?

If a 'whole school policy' on remedial education is merely a statement of aims and objectives, it is unlikely to be very effective. There are few schools which would not be willing to state, for example, that they are concerned to meet the needs of all pupils, no matter what their abilities and attainments. It is the translation of such aims into practice which matters. It would seem therefore that to be effective, such a policy would have to include more detailed agreement on the organisation of remedial provision and the deployment of remedial teachers and on the respective responsibilities of remedial teachers, subject teachers and management staff. An agreed policy framework - for example, that remedial teachers should work alongside subject staff, giving help where possible to pupils with learning difficulties in the ordinary classroom - would have a number of advantages. It would delineate some of the remedial teacher's (and subject teacher's) responsibilities and most importantly perhaps, it would legitimate the remedial teacher's involvement 'across the curriculum'. It might also encourage certain expectations of collaborative work and suggest that there are a number of alternative forms of provision which could be tried. Problematic issues such as terminology, identification and assessment could be discussed. This would have the advantage of not only possibly securing some measure of agreement on some of these issues but also of making staff aware of their complexity and difficulty. The development of a policy could also provide a forum for discussing the literacy and other demands made on pupils in lessons, or different approaches to the organisation of teaching, to try and secure more consistency of approach throughout the school. Agreement on staffing and resources in this area might also be useful, to safeguard and facilitate conditions for implementation of policy.

Given the diversity of views and practices within a school, and the range of professional interests which any policy is likely to challenge or support, there will inevitably be some conflict. It may only be possible at first to secure some general agreement on the remedial teacher's role, for example, with little agreement being reached on ways in which such new responsibilities will be realised. The 'bare bones' of such a policy will then have to be fleshed out with gradually negotiated agreements on ways of working with individuals and departments which may gradually become more formalised as agreed 'whole school policies'. It may well be the case that certain conflicts, about the organisation of teaching, or the power of remedial teachers to implement decisions reached, cannot be resolved. Are such conflicts then to be settled by fiat, with the remedial or headteacher making decisions or does a 'whole school policy' imply mutual agreement on all major issues? Given the emphasis on collaborative work within the redefinition of remedial education, it would seem preferable to build up a 'consensus' of negotiated agreements which can then form the basis of school policy. On the other hand, a fairly prescriptive policy, one which has perhaps been drawn up by a working party or group for discussion at departmental and staff meetings, could lay out guidelines to which practice could aspire and thus provide a sharper impetus to change. As with the 'partnership' between remedial and subject teacher, accounts of the development of 'whole school policies' could be usefully disseminated and discussed, accounts which gave details of how policies were agreed and what they comprised. This would help to elaborate and define what such policies may mean in relation to remedial education and how they could facilitate new approaches to provision. Such policies may well legitimate the remedial teacher's cross-curricular role and provide collegial support, but if they are going to be an important element of redefining remedial education, then they should be given more consideration and not just be put forward as a relatively unproblematic vehicle for change.

TERMINOLOGY, IDENTIFICATION AND ASSESSMENT

The categories and constructs associated with learning difficulties and remedial teaching are one of the most crucial aspects of remedial education. Equally they are particularly problematic. A wealth of discussion and research has centred on the issues of terminology, definition, incidence, identification and assessment. Yet despite the plethora of tests, surveys and research, there are still no absolute or functional definitions of what constitutes a learning difficulty, or to use the terminology of the Warnock Report and the 1981 Education Act, a 'special educational need'. The survey of research carried out for the Warnock Committee (Cave and Maddison,1978) reported on a range of difficulties associated with identification, assessment and estimates of incidence, difficulties which had arisen because of the lack of agreed criteria for definition, the relativities associated with differences in educational provision and the range of terminology employed. Nevertheless the Warnock Report, on the basis of a number of surveys, did suggest that some 20% of the school population might be considered to have 'special educational needs' at some time during their school career. No attempt was made however to put forward specific criteria within the Report or in the ensuing legislation of the 1981 Education Act. This Act defined a child with special educational needs as having a 'significantly greater difficulty in learning than the majority of children of his age' or having a disability 'which either prevents or hinders him from making use of educational facilities of a kind generally provided in schools' (Section One).

Such definitions and the absence of specific criteria may pose particular problems for remedial teachers or special needs teachers as they may increasingly be called. As NARE has commented, whereas handicapped pupils may have their needs recognised, the less obvious cases, such as pupils with mild learning difficulties may raise considerable problems of definition. Phrases such as 'significantly greater' or 'the majority of children' could lead to differences of interpretation and thus of provision (1985,p.6). So much may depend on the curriculum and organisation of the school or on the beliefs and attitudes of those making the decisions. Even if definition could be agreed, which is unlikely given the non-normative nature of the category of 'remedial pupil' or 'pupil with learning difficulties' or 'special educational need', the issue of terminology has also to be considered. Whatever the term used, all would seem to have some stigmatising connotations[8]. Nevertheless whatever the problems involved, remedial or special needs teachers will have to make some decisions about definitions, terminology, identification and assessment in order to develop policy and provision within a school.

Given the diversity of policies, provision and practice, including the possibility that some schools will be involved in the integration of pupils who might otherwise have gone to special schools, the choice of terminology will probably have to be an individual school decision. Some schools may well not wish to differentiate between 'remedial' and other forms of 'special' provision and may thus prefer to use the term 'special educational needs' for all pupils considered to have some form of learning difficulty or disability or handicap. Where the legislative framework of the 1981 Education Act may be used to encourage the development of new approaches to remedial education and to stress the duty of schools to provide for pupils with difficulties, the use of the Act's term, namely 'special educational needs' may be a useful strategy. At the same time, the stigmatising connotations of such a term needs to be minimised, and the concept of 'need' has to be carefully defined[9]. Booth's argument (1983b,p.4) that special needs are 'unmet needs', that it is the curriculum and organisation which should change, may provide a less stigmatising and less 'deficit based' touchstone for definition and also offers a useful basis for developing cross-curricular work to effect such changes. Terms such as 'learning adviser' for 'remedial teacher' or instead of 'special needs teacher', or perhaps, 'support teacher', would also seem to have the advantage of directing attention away from the problems of pupils towards the problems of the curriculum and the organisation of the school, and seem to stress the positive ('learning' and 'support') aspects of intervention rather than the more negative ones of 'remedying' 'deficits' and 'difficulties'.

If the issue of terminology was an element of the 'whole school policy' on remedial/special provision this might encourage a more consistent approach, and discourage continued use of often inaccurate and stigmatising terms such as 'less able' or 'slow learner'. Equally, problems of definition could be raised as 'whole school policy' matters, since definition is likely to affect the extent and quality of provision, including resources, and the content and focus of remedial and collaborative work. Although, as has been noted, it does seem to be extremely difficult to define what constitutes a 'learning difficulty' or a 'special educational need', due to the non-normative nature of such categories, discussion of the problems of definition might make teachers more aware of the many issues involved. It would also facilitate greater knowledge and understanding of subject teachers' constructs of learning difficulties, which, it has been previously argued, may be a pre-requisite to successful collaborative work between remedial and subject teacher.

Such discussion could be allied to the development of assessment procedures more appropriate to 'remedial education across the curriculum'. It has been suggested in previous chapters that traditional assessment of pupils with learning difficulties has been concerned primarily with the 'basic skills' of literacy and to a lesser degree, numeracy. Although our current knowledge of subject teachers' constructs of learning difficulties and of problems experienced by pupils in subject lessons cannot be regarded as definitive, from my own research and the available literature, it could be suggested that a far more sensitive conception of learning difficulties needs to be developed which would take into account the skills and knowledge required in different subject areas and how such demands may influence perceptions of pupil performance. Equally the skills and characteristics required of pupils by different modes of teaching, and the influence which such modes of teaching may have on subject teachers' perceptions of learning problems needs to be more carefully considered and incorporated into the process of assessment. Such developments could perhaps be further aided by the adoption of criterion-based procedures which would look at such skills, knowledge and characteristics, and at the demands made on pupils in lessons, and thus facilitate more detailed assessments of which pupils do actually need help and in what respect. A further and extremely valuable consequence of such an approach could be the discussion generated about the demands made on pupils, which could encourage recognition of the need for curricular and pedagogical changes to accommodate pupils who might have particular difficulties or lack certain skills, and thus better facilitate their learning.

It is unlikely that such assessment procedures would completely change the comparative nature of most assessment. As noted in Chapter Three, even criterion-referenced testing still implicitly or explicitly recognises the achievements of other pupils. Given too, that comparison and selection are part of the current function of schools, comparative evaluation of pupil performance will continue to be made, both informally, during the ordinary course of teaching and more formally, through examinations. Nevertheless such an approach does offer alternative ways of thinking about pupil performance in relation to learning difficulties. It certainly could be seen as preferable to procedures which emphasise the differences between 'normal' and 'abnormal' performance or which may 'create' learning difficulties through assumptions about the normative spread of pupil attainments and abilities. It might also encourage consideration of pupils' strengths as well as their difficulties, across the curriculum, in contrast to more traditional forms of assessment which tend to focus on weaknesses in a very restricted area, in particular the problems of literacy.

Finally, although the incidence, and indeed definition of learning difficulties or 'special educational needs' may vary from school to school, according to school intake, provision and resources and the beliefs and interpretations of those involved in decision making and planning, there is one general issue which needs to be considered. The Warnock Report was welcomed for the recognition it gave, amongst other things, to the extent of 'special educational needs' in ordinary schools, since such recognition carried with it the possibility of additional resources and more definitive policies to give support to such pupils and their teachers in such schools. However such recognition has led to the expansion of special education, with the accompanying possibilities that more pupils may be stigmatised as 'special' and that differentiation between pupils may be more easily legitimated. Special educational provision may also be criticised on the grounds that it serves an ideological function, in that distinctions between 'normal' and 'special' pupils help to buttress beliefs that the education system is catering adequately for most pupils, with special arrangements being needed to be made only for those who are not 'normal'[10]. However, as Quicke has noted, criticism of special education does pose a dilemma, for

> whatever the ideological significance of SE structures, they do at least provide a firm, well established and easily recognisable hook

on which to hang resources.
(1981,p.62)

Thus to argue for integration, or criticise the expansion of special education, may lead to cut backs in resources, particularly if it is not recognised that integration requires additional expenditure or that pupils in ordinary schools, even if they are not deemed to be 'special', may still need a considerable input of staffing and resources. It is thus very tempting to argue the very great extent of 'special educational needs', in the hope or assumption that if the 'problem' gets big enough, it will attract the necessary attention and resources and cannot be easily dismissed. Nevertheless if special education is potentially stigmatising, and if its expansion will, as Tomlinson (1985) has suggested, provide an increasingly important mechanism for differentiation and a rationale and justification for the economic and social position of those unemployed young people who are not part of the academic and technical elite of a post-industrial, technologically based society, then the value of identifying more and more pupils as having 'special educational needs' has to be seriously questioned. Such questioning is even more important when despite such identification, resources are not forthcoming - the 1981 Education Act, for example, does little to safeguard, let alone increase, resources and provision for the majority of those pupils now deemed to have 'special educational needs'.

Thus whatever terminology is employed for pupils with learning difficulties, be it 'special educational needs' or otherwise, careful consideration should be given to the expansion of such categories of pupils[11]. Although such expansion may have the potential to attract resources, and may also sensitise both teachers and policy-makers to the extent of the 'problem' and the need to do something about it, its strategic value may be limited and indeed such expansion could be damaging. Apart from the serious issue of the function of such expansion in current society, there remains the possibility that it will deflect attention, through an emphasis on the 'special' nature and characteristics of pupils, away from those curricular and organisational features of schools which contribute to such learning difficulties or 'special educational needs'. Thus despite intentions to improve provision for such pupils, through the identification of the extent of problems in schools, there may be the unintended but very real consequence that one of the primary aims of redefining remedial education, namely curricular and organisational change, will be dissipated in a plethora of assessments which may well identify 'needs' but offer less in respect to changing some of their fundamental causes.

CURRICULAR AND ORGANISATIONAL CHANGE

How, then, should attention be directed towards such change and how might 'remedial education across the curriculum' be developed? The review, in Chapter Two, of some of the contributions to the redefinition of remedial education, summarised a number of suggestions, including the extension of the remedial teacher's role, the initiation of a 'new partnership' between remedial and subject teacher to share the expertise of the remedial teacher and give support to pupils with learning difficulties in mainstream classes, and the development of 'whole school policies' on provision. Much attention was also given in such contributions to the improvement of assessment, to the modification of teaching materials and methods, to staff development and to ensuring flexible organisation of remedial help. These new 'partnerships' and 'policies' have already been discussed. Some consideration will now be given to the focus of such developments, namely provision for pupils with learning difficulties across the curriculum.

The redefinition of remedial education seems to be primarily concerned with three aspects of change in such provision, namely changes in organisational structure, changes in curricular content and changes in teaching methods. Changes in organisational structure may include less reliance on extraction or withdrawal for remedial help, so that pupils with learning difficulties are primarily taught in mainstream classes. The remedial teacher's responsibility for such remedial tuition will not necessarily be abolished, but such traditional responsibilities will be meshed with a new involvement in mainstream teaching.

As noted in Chapter Four, such changes in the organisation of provision are not without problems. It was considered by the subject teachers whom I interviewed that although integration in mainstream lessons had a number of advantages for pupils, it could reduce the individual attention and close relationships afforded by small groups. It was also noted in Chapter Five that although pupils seem to generally prefer such integration, they can be 'shown up' in mainstream classes through failing to understand a teaching point or by being given the support of a remedial teacher. The provision of appropriate help without stigma will remain perhaps as an insoluble dilemma where 'solutions' may be no more than the 'best compromise' available. Choices will also have to be made in accordance with the specific difficulty being encountered. However consultation with teachers, pupils and parents would seem to be an important element of any policy and decision, and at least the framework of policy and organisation could be altered, so that the principle is integration, and arguments have to be made for extraction, rather than the opposite which has often tended to be the pattern. Then the purpose and benefit of any withdrawal would have to be clearly considered and outlined, and it would not necessarily be assumed that certain difficulties should inevitably require extraction.

In respect to changes in the curriculum, one of the major arguments of this book has been concerned with the need to refocus the 'diagnostic skills' of remedial teachers. Knowledge of assessment and teaching techniques to overcome difficulties with basic skills will continue to be important. However, with the redefinition of remedial education, the contexts in which such difficulties may be experienced will also have to be considered and subject syllabi, materials and teaching methods will also be a focus of the remedial teacher's expertise as 'remedial education across the curriculum' is developed. The modification of materials, the development of a variety of teaching techniques and resources and new ways of organising learning in mainstream subject lessons may all be part of a 'new partnership' between remedial and subject teacher. Such work may involve assessment of the difficulty and suitability of curriculum materials, examination of the range of teaching materials and strategies which have been suggested in connection with subject teaching and pupils with learning difficulties, the preparation of materials and lessons which will develop both basic skills such as reading and also facilitate the learning of subjects and consideration of suitable methods of grouping and teaching pupils with different needs in mainstream classes.

It has also been suggested in previous chapters that some consideration needs to be given to the implications of curricular and organisational change. For example, although the modification of teaching materials to accommodate and overcome learning difficulties may facilitate participation and learning, care needs to be taken to ensure that difficulties, such as those with reading or writing, are not avoided and that opportunities for skill development are provided. Equally, when concepts or ideas are simplified, such simplification should not prevent, where possible, pupils 'engaging' with what is considered to be the most important aspects of a subject. Thus there will be certain dilemmas to resolve when modifying materials. Consideration will also have to be given to the possibility that such modifications will further differentiate those pupils who have learning difficulties. Finding the 'balance' between work which pupils may find too difficult and providing easier activities which may then proclaim the pupil to be 'different' is not easy. But given that such differentiation may not only 'show up' a pupil but may also prevent certain future curriculum choices because work covered in the past has been too narrow or simple, it does seem that where possible, efforts should be directed towards providing common curricular experiences for all pupils. If integration and participation in the common curriculum are seen to be desirable for pupils with learning difficulties, then such integration needs to be more than sitting in the same room or lesson. There has to be integration in terms of what pupils actually learn and experience.

The overall organisation and management of teaching and learning in the mainstream classroom may also pose certain problems and dilemmas. Although it could be suggested that a system of individual learning is most likely to facilitate effective provision for pupils with learning difficulties, in that work can be matched to pupil needs, differences in work set may not be so obvious if all pupils are working on different tasks and remedial support can be easily and flexibly deployed, such a mode of organisation does raise certain issues. The more commonly used system of individuated learning, where pupils proceed at their own pace, may result in pupils with learning difficulties never fully completing work, so that differences in what has been learned, between different pupils, may be great and if the work set is not organised well, what is learned by 'slower' pupils may be both disjointed and distorted. Individualised learning makes great demands on resources and teacher time, and there still remains the problem of differentiation, coupled with the possibilities of academic and social isolation that can accompany an individually-based system. On the other hand, whole class teaching or even group work can create difficulties for some pupils in terms of understanding and participation, even though such methods have the advantages of providing some common and social experiences of learning. Again, it perhaps has to be recognised that all forms of organisation have their accompanying advantages, disadvantages and dilemmas and that a judicious mix of approaches might be most appropriate. Certainly it cannot be assumed that any one approach provides a panacea and will effectively cater for 'individual need'. As was argued in Chapter Three, such an assumption, particularly in relation to promulgation of 'individual' approaches as the prime mode of 'good practice', may, if the limitations and constraints upon such practice are not realised, result in the learning difficulties of pupils, rather than the teaching difficulties of teachers, being seen as the sole source of problems.

Thus the processes and issues involved in curricular and organisational change raise a number of questions which are not easy to resolve. The initiation and maintenance of such change may be equally difficult. However a number of issues have been discussed in previous chapters which could be considered in relation to particular schools. For example, is subject and professional autonomy highly valued in the school or would teachers be willing to engage in collaborative work, perhaps drawing from previous experiences of team teaching? What are the major dimensions of subject teachers' constructs of pupils with learning difficulties - are they concerned about basic skills, intellectual abilities or learning and behavioural characteristics such as concentration or motivation? What too are their main pedagogical concerns and how do they perceive the problems of classroom management? Are they mostly concerned about lack of teacher time, about their expertise in relation to pupils with learning difficulties or about managing the range of ability and pacing within the class? And what demands are made of pupils within subject lessons in respect to skills, knowledge and characteristics required in different subjects and in modes of their transmission? Are traditional responsibilities for withdrawal tuition and assessment likely to impinge on the time available for cross-curricular work? Can assessment procedures be modified to support the development of such work? And is support for innovation likely to be forthcoming from the Headteacher and other management staff?

Such an informal schedule or checklist of questions, which could well be further elaborated or modified to include other issues which have been discussed in this book or elsewhere, could perhaps be used as a starting point for examining the 'readiness' (to borrow yet another analogy from remedial practice) of a school for innovation in remedial education and may also help to identify the possible sources of problems which may later be encountered during implementation. It might also suggest the strategies which could be adopted during the course of developing new approaches. This may involve not only considering whether such strategies should broadly be 'rational-empirical', 'normative-reeducative' or possibly even 'power-coercive', as discussed earlier in this chapter, but also considering where collaborative work might best be initiated and developed and how. For example, if there are teachers who are dissatisfied with current practice, who attempt to already make some provision for pupils with difficulties and do not seem to be particularly concerned to closely guard their autonomy, then collaborative work might best be initiated and developed with them to start with, as opposed to with teachers who do not seem to feel that working with a remedial teacher to improve provision with pupils with learning difficulties is congruent with their self-image or professional responsibilities. A 'trial' with a small group of teachers in different departments or with one particularly interested department could be initiated, to develop experience of collaborative work within the school, generate consideration of some of the issues and problems which may be involved and to demonstrate the feasability and hopefully, the value of such an approach to provision for pupils with learning difficulties.

Whether collaborative work is introduced stage by stage, with different departments and teachers, or as a consequence of prior discussion and agreement through the school's decision making structures, investigation of subject teachers' particular concerns may also help to identify strategies for change. If subject teachers are, for example, apparently most concerned about their expertise in relation to pupils with learning difficulties, the remedial teacher's time and support might be most usefully directed towards discussion and staff development, including workshops for interested teachers or individual sessions with teachers or departments. If on the other hand, teachers are particularly concerned about managing the range of ability and pacing within a class, or not having enough time to help pupils with learning difficulties, attention could probably be most usefully directed to those issues, explaining and demonstrating in practice how advisory and direct support work in class may help with these problems. Once such collaborative work has been established, where problems are encountered, it may be useful to consider the issues which may be involved. There may be some conflict over different views on subject content, or teaching methods, or some anxiety about professional autonomy. Alternatively the problem may be one of different interpretations of the purpose of such work - the subject teacher, for example, may consider that its prime purpose should be the 'solution' of classroom management problems such as lack of teacher time, and thus remedial teachers should use support work to give particular pupils more time and attention. The remedial teacher, on the other hand, may have another agendum, that of curricular change, and may thus wish to devote most time to modifying materials or teaching methods so that the subject teacher can provide more effectively for such pupils. Such differences in interpretation need gradually to be clarified and discussed, so that negotiation and agreement can take place. Otherwise, collaboration and the development of 'remedial education across the curriculum' may come to be regarded, by subject and remedial teacher, as 'impractical' or 'unworkable', but without an understanding of why problems are occurring and what could possibly be done about them.

To suggest that strategies for change should take cognisance of subject teachers' concerns and views is not to be 'manipulative' nor does it necessarily mean that the remedial teacher's own agenda need to be ignored. Given however, that the implementation of redefined remedial education is highly dependent on the views and practices of participants other than the remedial teacher, they cannot be ignored. As has been suggested throughout

this book, the processes of change involved in the
redefinition of remedial education are complex. The
issues which surround remedial education, together
with the legacies of past status and practice, in
themselves may be difficult enough to resolve. The
additional new involvement with teachers 'across the
curriculum' to forge new 'partnerships' and policies
within the whole school may be the only way of
realising a redefinition of remedial education but
at the same time it will bring new and further
problems for resolution.

In looking at the prospects for curricular and
organisational change and in examining the school,
the views of teachers and pupils, the problems of
provision and appropriate strategies, it will be
equally important to consider the remedial teachers
themselves. Are they aware of some of the problems
as well as the advantages of working across the
curriculum? Can they change their expertise? Are
they willing to consider different strategies and
approaches? Are they aware of some of the
implications of redefinition, both for themselves,
in terms of the stresses and career changes it may
bring, and for their pupils, in terms of the changes
which may occur in their learning and social
experiences? Can they be sensitive to others'
'definitions of the situation'? And are they indeed
convinced of the value and effectiveness of a new
approach? In becoming agents of curricular and
organisational change in schools, remedial teachers
ought not to ignore the importance of being 'change
agents' in respect to their own beliefs, expertise
and practice.

A more analytical approach to the redefinition
of remedial education may therefore help the
effective use of opportunities which are available
for change. At the same time, the constraints of
time and staffing may limit the extent to which
collaborative work across the curriculum can be
developed. It was suggested in Chapters Four and
Five that insufficient remedial teachers and the
consequent lack of time and staff to develop such
work could well be one of the major reasons why new
approaches have not been implemented in schools.
Perhaps some consideration could be given therefore
to involving other members of staff, if they have
some time available on their timetables. The
remedial teacher's 'expertise' may not always be
required in support work and an additional teacher,
of whatever subject, could help with problems like
lack of teacher time to give sufficient attention to

pupils with learning difficulties. Or subject teachers within a department could decide to operate some form of team teaching, so that one teacher could focus on pupils having difficulties, or departments could share materials developed by the remedial teacher and one subject teacher, in order to spread the benefits of collaborative work. Alternatively, to 'free' remedial teachers for support and advisory work across the curriculum, other teachers could become involved in withdrawal groups, helping with reading, for example, particularly where such withdrawal teaching is considered to be necessary but is encroaching on the time available to the remedial teacher for cross-curricular work. 'Link' teachers in each department, with particular responsibility for provision for pupils with learning difficulties, could also be established, to facilitate liaison and continuity with the work of remedial teachers. Such involvement from subject teachers might also help to break down distinctions between remedial and mainstream provision and help to establish commitment from all teachers to curricular and organisational change for pupils with learning difficulties.

However, such approaches, however useful, will only provide limited solutions to the problems of staffing and resources. If indeed it is the case that such problems are seriously inhibiting the implementation of redefined remedial education, arguments for increases in staffing and resources need to become the major focus of policy debate. Changes in attitudes and in practice may be an important part of the redefinition of remedial education, but if those changes cannot be facilitated without further staffing and resources, then the financial implications of redefinition and its adoption as 'good practice' will need to be far more clearly argued. Given current financial stringencies and a political climate which stresses economic rather than educational priorities, this may mean remedial teachers having to become far more 'political' in their approach to change. It will have to be recognised that the former 'consensus' of social and educational policies, which amongst other things did endorse the use of education as a means of promoting and extending equality (Kogan,1978) has now been fragmented and eroded by the subservience of social to economic goals. Moreover, those economic goals are being pursued in a particularly harsh and inflexible manner which sees no alternative policies and goals as valid and has shifted responsibility for inequality from societal failure to individual culpability (Barton and Walker,1984). However many of the arguments surrounding the importance of remedial education and which may be put forward as rationales for its development and expansion are located in former policy frameworks and in particular, in the beliefs that inequality is in part a societal issue and responsibility and that positive discrimination should be available to help equalise educational outcomes and consequent life chances. Any pursuit of greater resources and improved provision for pupils with learning difficulties will thus require an engagement with the whole tenor of current government policies.

Thus given current stringencies on educational spending, which are seriously affecting the education of all pupils, let alone those with learning difficulties, and given the current emphases of government policies, it may be very difficult to achieve changes in remedial education. Moreover, in looking at the wider context of remedial education, as has been suggested in previous chapters, those changes in subject content and skills, in pedagogy, in policy priorities and in staffing and resources which would seem to be required to alter the basis on which learning difficulties are perceived and provided for, are unlikely to be immediately forthcoming. Certainly it cannot be assumed that the redefinition of remedial education will change, nor indeed even seriously challenge, the central importance of high status academic knowledge within the secondary school curriculum, or the material conditions of teaching or the comparative and selective functions of schools. Given too that remedial education is part of the processes through which schools reproduce existing social relations, providing both a legitimation and a structure for the continued inequalities of educational achievement, with working class and black pupils forming the majority of its clientele, it may well be that changes which challenge both that legitimation and those structures will not be easily achieved without more radical changes in society[12].

Thus the prospects for radical curricular and organisational change may well be limited. At the same time it has been suggested in this book that whatever the problems of instituting new approaches, and there may be many, the redefinition of remedial education may have some potential. It does posit the greater integration of remedial teachers and pupils within the mainstream of school life and may afford some concrete improvements in the curricular experiences offered to pupils with learning difficulties. It also appears to offer some benefits to both remedial and subject teachers, such as new 'coping strategies' for subject lessons and a more stimulating and central role for remedial teachers. Moreover, the redefinition of remedial education has changed the tenor of debate about learning difficulties, from an exclusive emphasis on the problems of pupils towards an emphasis on the need for curricular and organisational change. Now that the limitations of the 'ambulance service' have at least been recognised, the opportunities which are available can perhaps be more effectively utilised to develop comprehensive and egalitarian principles within secondary education and a concomitant improvement in provision for pupils with learning difficulties. And even if the diversity of remedial provision is likely to remain a characteristic feature and indeed may well be increased with the new involvement with a variety of subjects and teachers, the positing of a particular model of 'good practice' may at least provide a greater clarity as to the general aims of remedial education.

Thus if it is considered that provision for pupils with learning difficulties should reflect integrative and egalitarian principles and should be improved to offer them more opportunities to develop their skills and knowledge across the curriculum and if it is considered that the low status, inadequate resources and lack of policy attention traditionally accorded to remedial education is thus far from satisfactory, the redefinition of remedial education could be welcomed, in the light of the prospects, however limited, which it affords to implement such principles and improvements. Debate now needs to be focused on the ways in which such prospects could be realised, the problems which may be encountered, the policies and strategies which may minimise those problems and the consequences, beneficial or otherwise, which may occur from change. Such a focus has indeed been the aim of this book, in the hope that further debate and discussion will be generated. Particular attention has been given to the development of the role and the awareness of remedial teachers, who have been perceived within this redefinition, as agents of curricular and

166

organisational change. However the redefinition of
remedial education also posits changes in secondary
education and special education which cannot be
achieved by remedial teachers alone and should not
be, given the new emphasis on collaborative work
across the curriculum. This chapter will therefore
conclude with a brief consideration of how the
redefinition of remedial education and the broader
changes it posits could be given encouragement and
support from elsewhere.

SUPPORT FOR THE FUTURE

How then could other groupings and communities
within education usefully support change in remedial
education? Certainly if the concept of
'partnership' between remedial and subject teacher
is to be meaningful, the contribution of subject
teachers cannot be ignored and should be requested.
Within individual schools, subject teachers involved
in collaborative work are developing methods of
working with remedial teachers and a number of
subject specialists have written about the teaching
of their subject to pupils with learning
difficulties. Such research and accounts of
individual practice could be usefully developed
further, with, perhaps, some encouragement from
subject associations. Collaboration between
remedial and subject teacher in individual schools
could well be more fully reflected in closer liaison
between those subject associations and NARE[13]. Such
work could be further supported in initial and in-
service training, with subject advisers and teacher-
trainers working with their colleagues in
remedial/special education, to develop the expertise
of subject teachers, encourage contributions from
them about their experience and teaching methods in
relation to pupils with learning difficulties and to
give more information to remedial/special needs
teachers about the teaching of different subjects.
Joint meetings and courses could be organised, to
encourage discussion and the dissemination of
approaches developed in individual schools. Such
collaboration could also be further supported by the
establishment of resource centres, for both remedial
and subject teachers, which held examples of
collaborative work and of different policies within
schools. The collaboration between remedial and
subject communities could also be accompanied by
closer collaboration and liaison between special

needs teachers, including those in special schools, so that distinctions between 'mainstream' and 'special' schools are minimised.

The in-service training of remedial teachers will also have to be developed, to facilitate the redefinition of remedial education through the development of appropriate knowledge and expertise. Such training, and meetings of remedial teachers, could also help with the discussion and resolution of problems encountered in collaborative work. A number of suggestions have been made about appropriate in-service courses (e.g. NARE,1982, Gains,1985) which could well form the basis of such training.

There is also the question of local and national policy development. The 1981 Education Act has encouraged the elaboration and adoption of clearer policies towards special educational provision, including remedial education. Such policies should be readily available for all teachers to refer to and use for discussion and development of their own practice. A systematic programme of dissemination and discussion of such policies within LEAs would also be useful, as would be their wider dissemination, for discussion by those working in other LEAs. LEAs could also follow the example of ILEA, which has published the report of its committee set up to review special educational provision (ILEA,1985), a report which raises many issues of interest and importance to those concerned with such provision across the country. In respect to the development of national policies, HMI has produced some survey evidence and discussion on approaches to remedial provision in schools (e.g. DES,1984) but there is still a further need for more survey information and more discussion of policy and practice. It would, for example, be very useful to have more information on the numbers of schools now implementing new approaches, the advantages and disadvantages being encountered and the types of organisation and modes of practice which are being developed. Discussion on issues like 'whole school policies' could also be aided by greater dissemination of current practice, with perhaps some suggestions or examples of 'model policies' which could be or have been developed. Discussion on the secondary curriculum from HMI and the DES still too often pays little attention to the implications for provision for pupils with learning difficulties/special educational needs. Given that these pupils now deemed to have such 'needs' comprise one fifth of the school population, it would seem that they should be the focus of much more national policy attention, with some accompanying clear recognition of the staffing and resources implications of such policies.

There has been a small but steady growth in research interest in new approaches to remedial and special education. However as has been frequently noted in previous chapters, many questions and issues cannot be easily resolved because of insufficient research. Many areas of possible and useful research have been suggested in this book and hopefully it has been demonstrated that this area of provision has both intrinsic interest and value and raises issues pertinent to other aspects of education. Remedial/special education has been well supported by research on assessment, on learning difficulties and on teaching techniques but has been rather neglected by other communities of researchers, such as those concerned with educational policy, the curriculum and the sociology of education. Given that remedial/special education is an important and significant part of the education system which may be increasingly involved with 'mainstream' education, it can no longer be ignored.

Finally, there has been considerable debate about the current and future direction and practices of secondary education. Comprehensive schools are facing many problems and changes, due to youth unemployment, curricular contractions, cuts in expenditure, pupil disaffection, proposed new examinations, central government intervention in the curriculum and pressures to respond to social and technological change. The comprehensive and egalitarian principles of secondary education, which have always been somewhat precarious, are being further undermined by such problems and changes so that it could be argued that comprehensive schools are facing a 'crisis' (Ball,1984). Nevertheless some new approaches to secondary education are being mooted which posit the development of the common curriculum, the integration of subjects, new forms of assessment such as profiles, a new emphasis on personal and social education and on the processes of learning and the widening of concepts of achievement to include social, practical, aesthetic and cultural attainments and skills as well as cognitive attainments[14]. Such developments have a number of implications for remedial provision which need to be widely discussed by both remedial

educators[15] and by all of those involved in
secondary education, to ensure that they do
facilitate the greater integration of pupils with
learning difficulties within the curricular and
organisational mainstream of the school and do aid
the changes posited for schools by the redefinition
of remedial education[16].

The redefinition of remedial education does
involve many issues, problems and dilemmas which
need to be resolved. Its implementation will also
require a critical and sensitive understanding of
the many complex processes and views which may be
involved. The prospects for radical change may be
limited, but with such understanding, and an
awareness that the issues and problems encountered
are not just particular to individual situations but
may be common to many remedial teachers and their
schools, and thus need wide discussion, we can at
least try to ensure that the opportunities for
change which are available are used effectively, to
facilitate some redefinition of remedial provision
and of its wider context of secondary education.

NOTES

1. e.g. Gains (1976).
2. However the approach used usually posits an
'interaction' between individual disability or
difficulty and the environment, treating these two
'variables' as analytically distinct and thus not
recognising that the 'individual problem' may itself
be a social product.
3. See Chapter Three for a review of some of
this literature.
4. McCall (1983) offers many useful
suggestions on grouping for special needs.
5. The redefinition of remedial education,
with its emphasis on collaboration and the sharing
of expertise could perhaps be regarded as an example
of the 'normative-reeducative' approach. However
'rational-empirical' strategies may also be used,
when for example, the benefits of redefinition and
its value to pupils are being argued. The low
status of remedial teachers may prevent effective
use of 'power-coercive' strategies although they can
be discerned in arguments about the importance of
headteacher support and in suggestions that remedial
teachers should have a high status, management role.
The analysis of change strategies in remedial
education might clarify which strategy is being
used, and why, and what approaches are actually most

effective.
     6. See Robinson (1981) and Woods (1983) for summaries of much of this research and analysis.
     7. e.g. Barton and Tomlinson (1981,1984), Tomlinson (1982).
     8. The term 'special educational need' may be seen to be preferable to 'remedial' or 'slow learner', traditional terms which imply deficits in pupils. However the use of the term 'special' still implies that the pupil is not 'normal' and given the stigma often attached to handicap and to special schools, its use in mainstream schools for a larger number of pupils may even be more stigmatising than traditional terms.
     9. See Bines (1984) for further discussion of the strategic potential and possible problems of the 1981 Act in relation to developing new approaches to remedial education.
     10. See Tomlinson (1982) for a more detailed critique of special education.
     11. There have to be some reservations therefore about the definition of learning difficulties now being mooted by NARE (1985) which suggests that pupils whose attainments are below the average of the peer group, or those pupils of general average or above average attainment with a below average attainment in one or more areas, ought to be considered to have learning difficulties. Such a definition could involve over half of the school population being considered to have 'special needs'.
     12. As noted in Chapter Three, the number of working class and black pupils receiving remedial education is rarely considered to be a problematic issue except in terms of the imputed relationship between socio-cultural background and learning difficulties. Space does not allow for detailed discussion of the ways in which, for example, remedial education may legitimate social inequalities by making them appear to be based on individual merit (or lack of it). However, if there is going to be a new emphasis on 'preventing' learning difficulties (and thus offering such pupils greater opportunities and more equal life chances), then the implications which such changes may have in terms of social inequalities and the degree to which such change may be constrained by definitions of abilities and knowledge, and of learning problems, which reflect the interests of dominant social groups will have to be more seriously examined.
     13. Collaboration between NARE and other

associations, notably the Mathematics Association and the Geographical Association, has been established and NARE is also a member of COSTA. However further collaboration and liaison 'across the curriculum' still needs to be developed.

14. See, for example, Hargreaves (1982) and ILEA (1984). Other LEAs are also considering and supporting similar approaches, further dissemination of which could be useful. Whether such approaches can indeed be successfully instituted in secondary schools is another question, for they pose very different definitions of knowledge and achievement to those currently held and wide changes in the comparative and selective functions and processes of schools. However given their particular implications for pupils with learning difficulties, they do need to be discussed.

15. Widlake (1983) has given a lot of consideration to the implications of social and educational change for remedial education, thus encouraging a wider framework of debate. Further contributions along these lines would be very useful.

16. In particular it will be important to ensure that the development of social and personal education, or wider concepts of achievement or vocational training and education projects such as TVEI are not just limited to certain pupils, thus creating a new 'bi-partism' in which pupils with learning difficulties and other low attainers are offered a social and vocational training/education whilst 'academic' examinations and courses are provided for other pupils, for this would negate the very integration and cross-curricular change suggested in the redefinition of remedial education.

BIBLIOGRAPHY

Adams, A. and Pearce, J. (1974) Every English Teacher, Oxford University Press, Oxford

Arkell, K. and Haley, T. (1978) 'Planning for the Less Able', Teaching Geography, 4, 2, 56-60

Bailey, T. J. (1979) 'Arithmetical Difficulties of Less Able Pupils in the Secondary School - Some Thoughts on Assessment and Remediation', Remedial Education, 14, 4, 204-210

Bailey, T. J. (1981) 'The Secondary Remedial Teacher's Role Redefined', Remedial Education, 16, 3, 132-6

Bailey, T. J. (1982) 'Mathematics in the Secondary School', in M. Hinson and M. Hughes (eds) Planning Effective Progress, Hulton/NARE, London

Ball, S. J. (1980) 'Mixed Ability Teaching: The Worksheet Method', British Journal of Educational Technology, 11, 1, 36-48

Ball, S. J. (1981) Beachside Comprehensive A Case-Study of Secondary Schooling, Cambridge University Press, Cambridge

Ball, S. J. (1982) 'Competition and Conflict in the Teaching of English: A Socio-historical Analysis', Journal of Curriculum Studies, 15, 1, 1-28

Ball, S. J. (1983) 'A Subject of Privilege: English and the School Curriculum 1906-35', in M. Hammersley and A. Hargreaves (eds) Curriculum Practice Some Sociological Case Studies, Falmer Press, Lewes

Ball, S. J. (1984) 'Introduction: Comprehensives in Crisis?' in S. J. Ball (ed) Comprehensive Schooling: A Reader, Falmer Press, Lewes

Ball, S. J. and Lacey, C. (1980) 'Subject Disciplines as the Opportunity for Group Action: A Measured Critique of Subject Sub-cultures', in P. Woods (ed) Teacher Strategies, Croom Helm, London

Barton, L. and Tomlinson, S. (1981) (eds) Special Education: Policy, Practices and Social Issues, Harper and Row, London

Barton, L. and Tomlinson, S. (1984) (eds) Special Education and Social Interests, Croom Helm, London

Barton, L. and Walker, S. (1984) 'Introduction' in L. Barton and S. Walker (eds) Social Crisis and Educational Research, Croom Helm, London

Bell, P. (1970) Basic Teaching for Slow Learners, Muller, London

Bennis, W. G., Benne, K. and Chin, R. (1969) The
Planning of Change, Holt, Rinehart and Winston,
New York
Berrill, R. (1982) 'The Slow Learner and the Gifted
Child', in M. Cornelius (ed) Teaching
Mathematics, Croom Helm, London
Bines, H. (1984) 'The 1981 Education Act and the
Development of Remedial Education in Secondary
Schools', Remedial Education, 19, 2, 73-77
Boardman, D. (1982) (ed) Geography with Slow
Learners, Geographical Association, Sheffield
Booth, M. (1980) 'Teaching Geography to Lower
Ability Children', Teaching Geography, 5, 3,
99-104
Booth, T. (1983a) 'Pupils with Learning Difficulties
in Scotland', in Eradicating Handicap, Unit 14,
Open University Course E241
Booth, T. (1983b) 'Integrating Special Education',
in T. Booth and P. Potts (eds) Integrating
Special Education, Blackwell, Oxford
Bowie, S. and Robertson, J. (1985) 'Cooperating in a
Mixed Ability Setting: A Curricular Approach to
Learning Difficulties', Remedial Education, 20,
3, 129-34
Boyd, B. (1985) 'Whole School Policies', Forum for
the Discussion of New Trends in Education, 27,
3, 79-81
Brennan, W. K. (1977) 'A Policy for Remedial
Education', in P. Widlake (ed) Remedial
Education: Programmes and Progress, Longman,
London
Brennan, W. K. (1979) Curricular Needs of Slow
Learners Schools Council Working Paper 63,
Evans/Methuen Educational, London
Brophy, J. E. and Good, T. L. (1974) Teacher Student
Relationships: Causes and Consequences, Holt,
Rinehart and Winston, New York
Bucher, R. and Strauss, A. (1976) 'Professions in
Process', in M. Hammersley and P. Woods (eds)
The Process of Schooling, Routledge and Kegan
Paul, London
Buckby, M. (1979) 'Teaching Pupils of Lower Ability
- Attitudes in the Classroom', Audio-Visual
Language Journal, 17, 2, 77-80
Burt, C. (1937) The Backward Child, Hodder and
Stoughton, London
Capron, A. C., Simons, A. and Ward, L. O. (1983)
'Principles for the Integration of Remedial
Pupils in the Comprehensive School', Remedial
Education, 18, 2, 75-80
Carrier, J. G. (1983) 'Explaining Educability: An

174

Investigation of Political Support for the Children with Learning Disabilities Act of 1969', _British Journal of Sociology of Education_, 4, 2, 125-40

Catling, S. (1984) 'Building Less Able Children's Map Skills', _Remedial Education_, 19, 1, 21-28

Cave, C. and Maddison, P. (1978) _A Survey of Recent Research in Special Education_, NFER, Slough

Chisholm, B. J. (1977) 'Remedial Help within Non-Streaming', _Forum for the Discussion of New Trends in Education_, 20, 24-6

Choat, E. (1974) 'Johnnie is Disadvantaged: Johnnie is Backward: What Hope for Johnnie?', _Mathematics Teaching_, 69, 9-13

Ciesla, M. J. (1979) 'Geography for Slow Learners in the Secondary School', _Remedial Education_, 14, 2, 64-68

Clark, M. M. (1976) 'Why Remedial? Implications of Using the Concept of Remedial Education', _Remedial Education_, 11, 1, 5-8

Clark, M. M., Barr, J. and McKee, F. (1982) _Pupils with Learning Difficulties in the Secondary School: Progress and Problems in Developing a Whole School Policy_, University of Birmingham/Scottish Council for Research in Education, Edinburgh

Clegg, A. S. and Morley, M. (1980) 'Applied Science - A Course for Pupils of Low Educational Achievement', _School Science Review_, 61, 216, 454-63

Cleugh, M. F. (1957) _The Slow Learner_, Aberdeen University Press, Aberdeen

Clunies-Ross, L. and Wimhurst, S. (1983) _The Right Balance: Provision for Slow Learners in Secondary Schools_, NFER/Nelson, Windsor

Collins, J. E. (1953) 'Remedial Educational Provision for Children of Average or Above Average Intelligence', _Educational Review_, 6, 2, 133-36

Collins, J. E. (1972) 'The Remedial Education Hoax', _Remedial Education_, 7, 3, 9-10

Cooper, B. (1983) 'On Explaining Change in School Subjects', _British Journal of Sociology of Education_, 4, 3, 207-222

Cooper, B. (1985) _Renegotiating Secondary School Mathematics_, Falmer Press, Lewes

Cooper-Maggs, R., Hardie, W. I. and Kirby, D. G. (1983) 'Teaching Geography to Lower Ability Pupils, Ages 12-14', _Teaching Geography_, 9, 1, 6-9

Corney, G. and Rawling, E. (1982) _Teaching Geography_

to Less Able 11-14 Year Olds, Geographical
Association, Sheffield

Corney, G. and Rawling, E. (1985) (eds) Teaching
Slow Learners Through Geography, Geographical
Association, Sheffield

Cowie, E. (1980) History and the Slow Learning
Child, Historical Association, London

Creber, J. P. W. (1984) Lost for Words, Classical
Press, Bristol

Croll, P., Moses, D. and Wright, J. (1984) 'Children
with Learning Difficulties and Assessment in
the Junior Classroom', in P. Broadfoot (ed)
Selection, Certification and Control: Social
Issues in Educational Assessment, Falmer Press,
Lewes

Dallas, D. (1980) Teaching Biology Today,
Hutchinson, London

Daniels, E. (1984) 'A Suggested Model of Remedial
Provision in a Comprehensive School', Remedial
Education, 19, 2, 78-83

Denscombe, M. (1980) 'Keeping 'Em Quiet: The
Significance of Noise for the Practical
Activity of Teaching', in P. Woods (ed) Teacher
Strategies, Croom Helm, London

Denvir, B., Stolz, C. and Brown, M. (1982) Low
Attainers in Mathematics 5-16 Schools Council
Working Paper 72, Methuen, London

DES (1971) Slow Learners in Secondary Schools
Education Survey 15, HMSO, London

DES (1975) A Language for Life (Bullock Report),
HMSO, London

DES (1977) Curriculum 11-16, HMSO, London

DES (1978) Special Educational Needs (Warnock
Report), HMSO, London

DES (1979) Aspects of Secondary Education in
England, HMSO, London

DES (1981) The School Curriculum, HMSO, London

DES (1982) Mathematics Counts (Cockcroft Report),
HMSO, London

DES (1984) Slow Learning and Less Successful Pupils
in Secondary Schools, DES, London

DES (1985a) Report by Her Majesty's Inspectors on
the Effects of Local Authority Expenditure
Policies on Educational Provision in England -
1981, DES, London

DES (1985b) The Curriculum from 5-16, HMSO, London

Duncan, A. (1978) Teaching Mathematics to Slow
Learners, Ward Lock, London

Dyson, A. (1983) 'Giants and Pygmies: An Approach to
Mathematics with Less Able Students in a
Secondary School', Mathematics in School, 12,

3, 10-12

Edwards, A. D. and Furlong, V. (1978) The Language of Teaching, Heinemann, London

Edwards, J. B. (1983) 'Remedial Education Post-Warnock: Interment or Revival?', Remedial Education, 18, 1, 9-15

Esland, G. M. (1971) 'Teaching and Learning as the Organisation of Knowledge', in M. F. D. Young (ed) Knowledge and Control, Collier and MacMillan, London

Evans, J. (1985) Teaching in Transition The Challenge of Mixed Ability Groupings, Open University Press, Milton Keynes

Evans, R. (1979) 'Identification and Assessment', in C. W. Gains and J. A. McNicholas (eds) Remedial Education: Guidelines for the Future, Longman, London

Ferguson, N. and Adams, M. (1982) 'Assessing the Advantages of Team Teaching in Remedial Education: The Remedial Teacher's Role', Remedial Education, 17, 1, 24-31

Flude, M. (1974) 'Sociological Accounts of Differential Educational Attainment', in M. Flude and J. Ahier (eds) Education, Schools and Ideology, Croom Helm, London

Furlong, V. J. (1977) 'Anancy Goes To School: A Case Study of Pupils' Knowledge of their Teachers', in P. Woods and M. Hammersley (eds) School Experience, Croom Helm, London

Gains, C. W. (1976) 'Mastery Learning and its Implications for Remedial Teachers', Remedial Education, 11, 1, 25-26

Gains, C. W. (1980) 'Remedial Education in the 1980s', Remedial Education, 15, 1, 5-9

Gains, C. W. (1985) 'Remedial Education: The Challenge for Trainers', in C. J. Smith (ed) New Directions in Remedial Education, Falmer Press, Lewes

Gains, C. W. and McNicholas, J. A. (1981) 'Broader Remedies', Times Educational Supplement, 11.9.81

Galletley, I. (1976) 'How to Do Away with Yourself', Remedial Education, 11, 3, 149-52

Goffman, E. (1959) The Presentation of Self in Everyday Life, Doubleday, New York

Golby, M. and Gulliver, R. J. (1979) 'Whose Remedies, Whose Ills? A Critical Review of Remedial Education', Journal of Curriculum Studies, 11, 137-47

Goodson, I. F. (1983) School Subjects and Curriculum Change, Croom Helm, London

Goodson, I. F. and Ball, S. J. (eds) (1984) Defining the Curriculum: Histories and Ethnographies, Falmer Press, Lewes

Gordon, M. (1983) 'Because They're Better Than Us! Planning for Failure in the Secondary School', Remedial Education, 18, 4, 174-7

Gough, B. and McGhee, J. (1977) 'Planning for Mixed Ability', in B. Davies and R. G. Cave (eds) Mixed Ability Teaching in the Secondary School, Ward Lock, London

Gray, J. (1981) 'Towards Effective Schools: Problems and Progress in British Research', British Educational Research Journal, 7, 1, 59-68

Gray, J., McPherson, A. F. and Raffe, R. (1983) Reconstructions of Secondary Education: Theory, Myth and Practice Since the War, Routledge and Kegan Paul, London

Griffin, D. (1978) Slow Learners: A Break in the Circle, Woburn Press, London

Gulliford, R. (1979) 'Remedial Work Across the Curriculum', in C. W. Gains and J. A. McNicholas (eds) Remedial Education: Guidelines for the Future, Longman, London

Hagerty, J. and Hill, M. (1981) 'History and Less Able Children', Teaching History, 30, 19-23

Hallam, R. (1982) 'History', in M. Hinson and M. Hughes (eds) Planning Effective Progress, Hulton/NARE, London

Hammersley, M. and Woods, P. (1984) (eds) Life in School The Sociology of Pupil Culture, Open University Press, Milton Keynes

Hargreaves, D. H. (1967) Social Relations in a Secondary School, Routledge and Kegan Paul, London

Hargreaves, D. H. (1980) 'The Occupational Culture of Teachers', in P. Woods (ed) Teacher Strategies, Croom Helm, London

Hargreaves, D. H. (1982) The Challenge for the Comprehensive School, Routledge and Kegan Paul, London

Hargreaves, D. H., Hestor, S. K. and Mellor, F. J. (1975) Deviance in Classrooms, Routledge and Kegan Paul, London

Hawkins, E. (1974) 'Teaching Modern Languages to Less Able Pupils' from 'Proceedings of the National Course in Modern Languages, Dunblane, 1973', Modern Languages in Scotland, 4, 76-78

Herndon, J. (1972) How to Survive in Your Native Land, Bantam, New York

Hewison, J. (1982) 'Parental Involvement in the Teaching of Reading', Remedial Education, 17,

$\underline{4}$, 156-162

Hinson, M. (1982) 'Science', in M. Hinson and M. Hughes (eds) Planning Effective Progress, Hulton/NARE, London

Holbrook, D. (1965) English for the Rejected, Cambridge University Press, Cambridge

Hodkinson, P. (1977) 'Mixed Ability Teaching: How Can We Choose Appropriate Techniques?', Teaching Geography, 12, 3, 108-9

Holt, J. (1969) How Children Fail, Penguin, Harmondsworth

Hoyle, E. (1971) 'The Role of the Change Agent in Educational Innovation' in J. Walton (ed) Curriculum Organisation and Design, Ward Lock, London

Hull, J. (1978) 'Mixed Ability History: A Graded Worksheet Approach', Teaching History, 22, 33-35

Hull, J. (1980) 'Practical Points in Teaching History to Less Able Secondary Pupils', Teaching History, 28, 14-18

Hyde, T. (1984) 'Secondary Remedial Provision within One Metropolitan Authority' Remedial Education, 19, 2, 85-90

ILEA, (1984) Improving Secondary Schools (Hargreaves Report), ILEA, London

ILEA, (1985) Educational Opportunities for All? (Fish Report), ILEA, London

Jones, H. (1979) 'Editorial', Remedial Education, 14, 2, 59-62

Jones, R. (1972) 'The Mixed Ability Class', English in Education, 6, 1, 56-62

Keddie, N. (1971) 'Classroom Knowledge' in M. F. D. Young (ed) Knowledge and Control, Collier MacMillan, London

Kelly, D. B. (1981) 'Withdrawal for Remedial Help in Secondary School', Remedial Education, 16, 2, 67-71

Kemp, R. (1979) 'Teaching Strategies for the Less Able', Teaching Geography, 5, 2, 52-54

Kemp, R. (1981) 'Teaching Strategies for Mixed Ability', Teaching Geography, 7, 2, 58-59

Kershaw, I. and Scott, P. J. (1975) 'Science for Pupils of Low Educational Attainment', School Science Review, 56, 196, 449-63

King, R. (1983) The Sociology of School Organisation, Methuen, London

Knights, G. (1974) 'Mathematics and Slow Learning Children', Mathematics Teaching, 67, 14-16

Kogan, M. (1978) The Politics of Educational Change, Manchester University Press, Manchester

Langman, T. (1978) 'History' in M. Hinson (ed) Encouraging Results, MacDonald Educational, London

Larcombe, T. (1978) 'Mathematics 11-14' in M. Hinson (ed) Encouraging Results, MacDonald Educational, London

Larcombe, T. (1985) Mathematical Learning Difficulties in the Secondary School, Open University Press, Milton Keynes

Lawrence, D. (1973) Improved Reading Through Counselling, Ward Lock, London

Lawton, D. (1980) The Politics of the School Curriculum, Routledge and Kegan Paul, London

Layton, D. (1984) Interpreters of Science A History of the Association for Science Education, Murray/ASE, London

Leach, D. J. and Raybould, E. C. (1977) Learning and Behaviour Difficulties in School, Open Books, London

Lee, S. (1984) 'Out of Sight, Out of Mind', Times Educational Supplement, 3.2.84

Lewis, G. (1984) 'A Supportive Role at Secondary Level', Remedial Education, 19, 1, 7-12

Lewis, M. (1973) 'Teaching French to Slow Learners', Modern Languages in Scotland, 1, 81-90

Lovell, K., Byrne, C. and Richardson, B. (1963) 'A Further Study of the Educational Progress of Children Who Had Received Remedial Education', British Journal of Educational Psychology, 33, 3-9

McCall, C. (1983) Classroom Grouping for Special Need, National Council for Special Education, Stratford-upon-Avon

McIver, V. (1982) Teaching History to Slow Learning Children in Secondary Schools, Learning Resources Unit, Stranmillis College, Belfast

McNicholas, J. A. (1976) 'Aims of Remedial Education: A Critique', Remedial Education, 11, 3, 113-116

McNicholas, J. A. (1979) 'The Remedial Teacher as a Change Agent', in C. W. Gains and J. A. McNicholas (eds) Remedial Education: Guidelines for the Future, Longman, London

MacDonald, B. and Walker, R. (1976) Changing the Curriculum, Open Books, London

Mathieson, M. (1975) The Preachers of Culture, Allen and Unwin, London

Miller, A. (1981) 'Approaches to the Failing Reader: A Problem of Paradigm Competition', Remedial Education, 16, 2, 71-76

Milner, S. (1978) 'Some Pupil Attitudes and the

Practical Application of New Geography in Schools', Classroom Geographer, November 1978, 15-18

Moseley, D. (1975) Special Provision for Reading, NFER, Slough

Murray, A. L. (1980) 'A Teacher's View of Syllabus for Less Able Pupils in S3 and S4', Modern Languages in Scotland, 20, 52-59

NARE (1977) Guidelines No. 1 Report on In-Service Training, NARE, Stafford

NARE (1979) Guidelines No.2 The Role of Remedial Teachers, NARE, Stafford

NARE (1982) Guidelines No.4 In-Service Education for Remedial Teachers, NARE, Stafford

NARE (1983) Guidelines No.5 Choosing Curriculum Materials, NARE, Stafford

NARE (1985) Guidelines No.6 Teaching Roles for Special Educational Needs, NARE, Stafford

Nettleship, J. (1972) 'From the Sublime to the Concrete', Remedial Education, 7, 2, 5-7

NUT (1980) Promotion and the Woman Teacher, National Union of Teachers, London

Pollard, A. (1980) 'Teacher Interests and Changing Situations of Survival Threat in Primary School Classrooms', in P. Woods (ed) Teacher Strategies, Croom Helm, London

Quicke, J. (1981) 'Special Educational Needs and the Comprehensive Principle: Some Implications of Ideological Critique', Remedial Education, 16, 2, 61-67

Raleigh, M. (1978) 'Mixed Ability English', English in Education, 12, 1, 53-62

Reid, M., Clunies-Ross, L., Goacher, B. and Vile, C. (1981) Mixed Ability Teaching: Problems and Possibilities, NFER/Nelson, Windsor

Reynolds, D. (1985) 'The Effective School', Times Educational Supplement, 20.9.85

Richmond, R. C. (1985) 'Recent Influences on the Assessment of Reading Difficulties and the Concept of Specific Difficulties', in C. J. Smith (ed) New Directions in Remedial Education, Falmer Press, Lewes

Robinson, P. (1981) Perspectives in the Sociology of Education An Introduction, Routledge and Kegan Paul, London

Rudduck, J. (1980) 'The National Association for the Teaching of English', in L. A. Stenhouse (ed) Curriculum Research and Development in Action, Heinemann, London

Rutter, M., Maughan, B., Mortimore, P. and Ouston, J. (1979) Fifteen Thousand Hours: Secondary

Schools and their Effects on Children, Open
Books, London
Sampson, O. C. (1975) Remedial Education, Routledge
and Kegan Paul, London
Sampson, O. C. and Pumfrey, P. D. (1970) 'A Study of
Remedial Education in the Secondary Stage of
Schooling', Remedial Education, 5, 3/4, 102-111
Schonell, F. J. (1942) Backwardness in the Basic
Subjects, Oliver and Boyd, Edinburgh
SED (Scottish Education Department), (1978) The
Education of Pupils with Learning Difficulties
in Primary and Secondary Schools in Scotland: A
Progress Report, HMSO, Edinburgh
Senior, P. H. (1979) 'Science for Slow Learners:
Some Personal Observations', Remedial
Education, 14, 3, 121-124
Sewell, G. (1982) Reshaping Remedial Education,
Croom Helm, London
Shayer, D. (1972) The Teaching of English in Schools
1900-1970, Routledge and Kegan Paul, London
Shayer, M. and Adey, P. (1981) Towards a Science of
Science Teaching, Heinemann, London
Smith C. J. (1982) 'Helping Colleagues Cope - A
Consultant Role for the Remedial Teacher',
Remedial Education, 17, 2, 75-79
Smith, D. G. (1973) 'French and the Less Able',
Modern Languages, 54, 4, 105-115
Spradbery, J. (1976) 'Conservative Pupils? Pupil
Resistance to Curriculum Innovation in
Mathematics', in G. Whitty and M. F. D. Young
(eds) Explorations in the Politics of School
Knowledge, Nafferton, Driffield
Stockwell, F. J. (1975) 'Remedial Mathematics',
Mathematics in School, 4, 6, 29-30
Stratta, L. (1965) 'English for Whom?' NATE
Bulletin, 2, 3
Sturges, L. M. (1973) 'Problems in Teaching Science
to Non-Streamed Classes', School Science
Review, 55, 191, 224-232
Tansley, A. E. (1967) Reading and Remedial Reading,
Routledge and Kegan Paul, London
Tomlinson, S. (1982) A Sociology of Special
Education, Routledge and Kegan Paul, London
Tomlinson, S. (1985) 'The Expansion of Special
Education', Oxford Review of Education, 11, 2,
157-165
Westbury, I. (1973) 'Conventional Classrooms, "Open"
Classrooms and the Technology of Teaching',
Journal of Curriculum Studies, 5, 2, 99-121
Westwood, P. (1975) The Remedial Teacher's Handbook,
Oliver and Boyd, Edinburgh

Widlake, P. (1975) 'Remedial Education at the Crossroads' and 'The Future in Remedial Education', Presidential Address and Concluding Remarks to NARE Conference, 1975, Remedial Education, 10, 3, 103-7

Widlake, P. (1983) How to Reach the Hard to Teach, Open University Press, Milton Keynes

Williams, A. (1970) Basic Subjects for the Slow Learner, Methuen, London

Williams, A. (1985) 'Towards Success in Mathematics', in C. J. Smith (ed) New Directions in Remedial Education, Falmer Press, Lewes

Williams, M. (1982) 'Geography' in M. Hinson and M. Hughes (eds) Planning Effective Progress, Hulton/NARE, London

Wilson, M. D. (1982a) 'The History Curriculum for Slow Learners', Teaching History, 32, 11-13

Wilson, M. D. (1982b) 'Teaching History to Slow Learners. Problems of Language and Communication', Teaching History, 33, 22-27

Wilson, M. D. (1982c) 'The Attitudes of Slow Learning Adolescents to the Teaching and Study of History, Teaching History, 34, 33-38

Woods, P. (1979) The Divided School, Routledge and Kegan Paul, London

Woods, P. (1983) Sociology and the School, Routledge and Kegan Paul, London

Young, M. F. D. (1971) 'An Approach to the Study of Curricula as Socially Organised Knowledge', in M. F. D. Young (ed) Knowledge and Control, Collier MacMillan, London

AUTHOR INDEX

Young, M. F. D. 6